AQA English Literature A

A2

Exclusively endorsed by AQA

Stella Canwell
Jane Ogborn

Nelson Thornes

Published in 2008 by:
Nelson Thornes Ltd
Delta Place
27 Bath Road
CHELTENHAM
GL53 7TH
United Kingdom

10 11 12 13 14 / 10 9 8 7 6 5 4 3 2

A catalogue record for this book is available from the British Library

ISBN 978 0 7487 8295 6

Cover photograph: Photolibrary/Digital Vision
Page make-up by Pantek Arts Ltd, Maidstone, Kent
Printed and bound in China by 1010 Printing International Ltd

Contents

AQA introduction

Nelson Thornes and AQA

Nelson Thornes has worked in partnership with AQA to ensure this book and the accompanying online resources offer you the best support for your A level course.

All resources have been approved by senior AQA examiners so you can feel assured that they closely match the specification for this subject and provide you with everything you need to prepare successfully for your exams.

These print and online resources together **unlock blended learning**; this means that the links between the activities in the book and the activities online blend together to maximise your understanding of a topic and help you achieve your potential.

These online resources are available on **kerboodle!** which can be accessed via the internet at http://www.kerboodle.com/live, anytime, anywhere. If your school or college subscribes to this service you will be provided with your own personal login details. Once logged in, access your course and locate the required activity.

For more information and help visit
http://www.kerboodle.com

Icons in this book indicate where there is material online related to that topic. The following icons are used:

Learning activity
These resources include a variety of interactive and non-interactive activities to support your learning.

Research support
These resources include WebQuests, in which you are assigned a task and provided with a range of web links to use as source material for research.

Study skills
These resources support you in developing skills that are key for your course, for example, planning essays.

Analysis tool
These resources help you to analyse key texts and images by providing questions and prompts to focus your response.

When you see an icon, go to **Kerboodle** at **http://www. kerboodle.com/live**, enter your access details and select your course. The materials are arranged in the same order as the topics in the book, so you can easily find the resources you need.

How to use this book

This book covers the specification for your course and is arranged in a sequence approved by AQA. The book is divided into seven chapters, beginning in Chapter 1 with an introduction to the English Literature A A2 Specification and how you will be assessed. Chapter 2 explains your coursework tasks, whilst Chapter 3 takes you through the requirements for your examination. Chapters 4 to 6 cover the genres of poetry, prose and drama, introducing wider reading texts, tracing the development of the genre across time and fine-tuning your skills of analysis. Chapter 7 introduces a specimen examination paper where you can practise your skills and approach and identify where you might need to improve them.

Definitions of any words that appear in bold blue text can be found in the glossary at the back of this book.

The features in this book include:

Aims of the chapter:

At the beginning of each section you will find a list of learning objectives that contain targets linked to the requirements of the specification.

Modern language

Modern synonyms for terms that are not in regular use today. These will help you understand archaic and unfamiliar words in the extracts within this book.

Did you know?

Interesting facts to extend your background knowledge.

Links

Links to refer you to other areas of the book which cover the topics you are reading about.

Further reading

Suggestions for other texts that will help you in your study and preparation for assessment in English Literature.

Activity

Activities that develop the skills you will need for success in your English Literature course.

Questions

Questions that help to focus your reading of key extracts and prepare you for writing on extracts in the examination and in your coursework.

AQA Examination-style questions

Questions in the style that you can expect in your examination. You will find these in Chapter 7.

Summary

A summary of what is covered in this chapter of the book.

AQA examination questions are reproduced by permission of the Assessment and Qualifications Alliance.

1   Introduction

Aims of the chapter:

- reflects on how the AS course has prepared you for A2
- introduces the content and skills of the A2 course
- considers the philosophy of reading and meaning that underpins the Specification
- explores the choices you will need to make
- shows how you will be assessed.

Link

Other chapters will look at:

- how to succeed in the coursework unit (Chapter 2)
- how to approach the written paper (Chapters 3 and 7)
- how to manage your wide reading across all genres (Chapters 4, 5 and 6).

Your A2 English Literature A coursebook

This book has been written to help you to be as successful as possible in your A2 AQA English Literature Specification A examinations. It will introduce you to the relevant **subject matter** that you need to **know and understand** as well as to the **skills** you need to develop in order to **read, analyse, interpret and write** about your texts.

In this chapter, we are going to look at:

- the importance of the AS course as a foundation for A2
- the components of the A2 course
- the kinds of reading you will be doing
- the Assessment Objectives
- the assessment grid.

A short summary of the A2 course

The course consists of **two units** of work: one is assessed through **coursework** and the other through **written examination**.

For **Unit 3**, the written examination, you will need to read widely across the **genres** of prose, poetry and drama, as well as through **time** (from Chaucer to the present day). You and your teacher are responsible for choosing the texts you read; they will all have **love** (as expressed in human relationships) as a central theme. The examination will invite you to comment on a selection of unprepared extracts which reflect this theme.

For **Unit 4**, the coursework, you will write an extended essay about three texts. Again, you and your teacher will choose the three texts. The two key requirements in this unit are that one text must be a Shakespeare play, and that the three texts for the essay must be linked thematically. The theme will be of your choice; it may be entirely independent of Unit 3, or it may be linked to it.

There are no 'set texts' anywhere in your course, although, as we have just established, there are requirements that you need to meet.

Reflecting on AS

The AS course developed your skills as an 'autonomous critic' of English Literature by concentrating your studies on a particular area of literature or what we called a 'shared context'. All your reading and study was focused on one of the three following areas of study:

- Victorian Literature
- The Literature of World War One
- Modern Literature on the theme of The Struggle for Identity.

Within your chosen area of literature you studied:

- prose – fiction and non-fiction
- poetry

poetry

- drama
- the ways the 'shared context' affected the writing.

Stepping up to A2

At A2 you move from a study of literature within a particular shared context to the whole of English Literature. The four Assessment Objectives remain the same, but interpretation of them widens and deepens. The key ways that your studies are widened and deepened when you move from AS to A2 are shown in the following table.

At AS	At A2
Two short coursework essays	One extended comparative essay
A short coursework drama essay linked to wider reading	A detailed Shakespeare study linked thematically to two other texts in an extended essay
A short unprepared passage on the exam paper	A whole paper of unprepared extracts
Set texts and reading lists from which to choose	Free choices of texts as approved by the Moderator of the Board
Reading widely within the shared context	Reading widely across time, genre and gender

To summarise

There are no set texts in the A2 course – the texts for study (both whole texts and extracts) will be chosen by your teacher and you. The framework of the Specification set up by the Board establishes that you need to read across time, genre and gender, and within the theme of love for Unit 3 – but there are considerable freedoms here for you and your teacher to pursue.

The outcomes of the A2 course will be:

1 an extended piece of coursework writing on three thematically linked texts – a Shakespeare play and two other texts of any genre
2 your response to two questions on an examination paper requiring exploration and analysis of four unprepared texts on the theme of love.

In order to be successful, you need to establish an **overview** of English Literature from Chaucer to the present day, developing an understanding of the development of genre and of critical response through time, and of the influence of literary, cultural, social, political and historical contexts. The breadth and depth of your own reading will be the key to your success. So we will now focus on the **kind of reader** you need to be.

i The informed, independent reader

The aim of the course is to enable you to develop as an informed, independent reader and critic of literary texts.

As an informed, independent reader, you build a reading of a text through:

- careful and close reading of a text which provides you with appropriate and specific evidence to support your interpretation
- consideration and understanding of other possible readings
- research into the contexts of both reading and writing.

It is true to say that what is written on the page can always be interpreted in a number of ways. An informed reader does not ignore contradictory evidence or try to impose one specific and extreme interpretation on a text; s/he builds a coherent reading based on textual evidence. It is important not to try to make a text mean anything you want it to; there are interpretations of texts that it is impossible to support or sustain. There are, indeed, wrong or unconvincing answers. On the other hand, there are also no exclusively right answers since it is the reader who constructs meaning. The writer may choose and shape, but once the words are in the public domain, it is the reader, not the writer, who is the 'maker of meaning'.

The AQA English Literature A Specification provides you, the reader, with maximum opportunities for selecting your own reading within a supportive framework and for writing on a theme of your own choice in the coursework unit. The whole A2 course promotes and fosters the skills of research and independent study and is an excellent preparation for further study in higher education. We will move on to consider both **wide** and **close** reading, but first we need to look at the philosophy underpinning the Specification.

Reading for meaning

You will need to be **actively engaged** with your texts in order to develop **informed, personal responses**.

The Specification is built on a philosophy about reading and meaning that you need to understand and share.

We think that:

Reading:

- is an active process: the reader is the **active creator**, not a passive recipient of second-hand opinion – *you are the 'maker of meaning'*
- can never be 'innocent': all readings are historically, socially and individually specific – *you bring your own personal context and experience to the text*
- is not a single skill: some kinds of reading are more demanding than others – *think, for example, of the comparable difficulty of reading a Mills and Boon romance on the one hand, and a Jane Austen novel on the other.*

Meaning:

- for an individual reader, depends as much on what is brought to the text as upon what is contained within it – *your own experience will influence the way you read the text*
- will not necessarily be instantly accessible – *you may well need to research references and vocabulary, for example, before you can tease out meaning*
- will be different on different occasions, and changeable as a result of discussion and reflection – *when you reread a text, for example, you may find your response is different from your first reading; discussion with your peers and/or your teacher or reading a critical commentary may also influence and change your response to a text*
- can be multiple; different readings of a text can co-exist – *you need to be aware that some texts are ambiguous or capable of delivering multiple meanings and it is your own selection of and response to textual evidence that will determine your interpretation.*

Wide reading

Wide reading is crucial to your success. If you read widely throughout the course, you will:

▓ have ample opportunity to discover your own interests and enjoyment, developing your awareness of the ways you respond to and understand different kinds of writing

▓ have the knowledge and skills that enable you to make and explore connections, comparisons and contrasts

▓ be able to see different points of view, exploring the ways that different writers describe a similar experience or situation

▓ discover the different ways different writers choose to communicate with you, the reader, exploring choices of form, structure and language.

At AS, all your wider reading was based on a coherent collection of texts within a specific area of literature. Your wider reading at A2 will support your studies in a different way.

For Unit 4, the focus of your writing will be on your three chosen texts, but there is no doubt that your wider reading will help you in your preparation and in the choosing of the texts for your coursework essay.

For Unit 3, it will be essential for you to read widely across time, gender and genre in the **Literature of Love** so that you can approach the examination paper and its unprepared texts with confidence.

Keeping a record of your reading will be very important, especially as you will no doubt be dealing with a great many extracts as well as whole texts. We suggest that you keep a detailed **Reading Log**; at the end of the course this will provide a very useful revision tool. Another useful thing to do would be to place all your reading on the theme of love on a **Time Line**.

▣ ▣ Close reading

Not only is it crucial to read widely throughout the course, but, as at AS, you must also develop the skills of **close reading**. You will use these skills in every answer you write and they underpin the whole course.

Close reading of a text will enable you to **analyse** and **explore** a writer's techniques – his or her choices of form, structure and language – so that:

▓ you respond fully to meaning or possible meanings of the text

▓ you gain understanding of the ways texts work

▓ you find textual evidence to support your interpretation.

If you are one of those students who does **not** read closely, you will only be able to offer a **skimpy** reading of your texts, based on **unsupported assertion**. This sort of response will not earn you a pass at A Level. Neither is there any point in counting numbers of syllables, making exaggerated claims for **alliteration**, or setting out a pattern of rhyme (a b a b c c, for example) unless this research is part of an analysis or exploration of the ways the writer's choices make meaning for you.

When you are exploring a text, some of the questions you should be asking yourself are:

▓ What kind of text is this?

▓ When was this text written?

■ What is the subject matter?

■ Who is speaking and how does the writer use the idea of 'voice' in the text?

■ How does the writer use setting(s)?

■ How does the writer use ideas of time? (past, present, future)

■ How does the writer structure, organise and develop the ideas in the text?

■ Is there anything distinctive in the way the text is written? (structure, choices of vocabulary, sentence structures, variations in pace ...)

■ Are there any patterns, repetitions of key ideas or images, uses of contrast?

■ What kinds of language are used? (formal, informal, descriptive, dialogue and so on)

■ How has finding out more about the references and **allusions** in the text added to my understanding and interpretation?

■ Is the language all the same or does the writer use contrast?

■ What is the tone of the text?

■ What might be the writer's purpose(s) in this text?

All the answers to the questions need to be related to your interpretation of the text, to the making of meaning.

💡 ⓩ Your reading log and wider reading portfolio

These records are tools that we suggest will help you in your preparation for assessment in your English Literature A A2 course.

Reading log

You should keep a record, either handwritten or electronic, of all the texts that you read during your course. This should be a short profile of each text with key points to help you remember and make connections between texts. Here are some examples of useful information which you should include in your reading log:

■ Title of the text

■ Writer

■ Date of composition

■ Genre

■ Brief summary

■ Key theme(s)

■ Use of language, form and structure that stood out to you.

💡 *Wider reading portfolio*

To make your wide reading useful to you, you will need to find ways of organising and recording what you read. We suggest that you make active use of the **English Literature through time grid** on pp124–5 of this book. You will find the major writers referred to in this book already in position on it, and you should also use it to record the results of your research into the biographies of the writers you read, with their dates and a note of key texts. You should create a **wider reading portfolio**, which will be your personal collection of texts about love that you can classify and organise in any way you like:

■ by genre

■ by author – chronologically or alphabetically

■ **Link**

For more information on how to use the **English Literature through time grid**, see Chapter 3.

- by date
- by period
- by subject – classifying texts according to the different aspects of love you identify during your reading.

This portfolio will be an essential revision tool when you come to prepare for your written examination.

Assessment

As at AS, all your work for the course will be assessed against four **Assessment Objectives**. These are:

AO1   Articulate creative, informed and relevant responses to literary texts, using appropriate terminology and concepts, and coherent, accurate written expression (*your ability to use your knowledge and understanding, to focus on the task, and to express yourself appropriately*)

AO2   Demonstrate detailed critical understanding in analysing the ways in which structure, form and language shape meanings in literary texts (*your ability to explore the ways the writers' choices of form, structure and language influence the ways you interpret texts and make meaning*)

AO3   Explore connections and comparisons between different literary texts, informed by interpretations of other readers (*your ability to find links between the texts you read and to explore alternative readings*)

AO4   Demonstrate understanding of the significance and influence of the contexts in which literary texts are written and received (*your ability to assess where and how your texts fit into literary tradition*)

These four Assessment Objectives are used to measure your achievement throughout the Specification and are organised by your examiners into a marking grid which is used to assess every piece of your writing.

You and your teachers will be able to check your performance against the criteria in the grid.

- If your work has the features of **Band One** work – **inaccurate**, **irrelevant**, **assertive** – you will not be writing at the required standard for A Level.
- If your work is assessed as falling into **Band Two**, it is judged to be **narrative** and **descriptive** and rather **generalised** in its approach to text.
- If your work is assessed in **Band Three**, then it means that you are starting to **explore** and **analyse** the texts and presenting your work in a **coherent** fashion.
- If your work is assessed in **Band Four**, it is **coherent**, **cogent**, **mature** and **sophisticated** and worthy of the highest grade.

The assessment grid for A2

	Assessment Objectives			
	AO1 Articulate creative, informed and relevant responses to literary texts, using appropriate terminology and concepts, and coherent, accurate written expression	**AO2** Demonstrate detailed critical understanding in analysing the ways in which structure, form and language shape meanings in literary texts	**AO3** Explore connections and comparisons between different literary texts, informed by interpretations of other readers	**AO4** Demonstrate understanding of the significance and influence of the contexts in which literary texts are written and received
Band 1	Candidates characteristically: a communicate limited knowledge and understanding of literary texts b make few uses of appropriate terminology or examples to support their interpretations c attempt to communicate using inaccurate language d present an unclear line of argument e make unsupported assertions.	Candidates characteristically: a identify few aspects of structure, form and language in literary texts b make limited references to texts to support their responses.	Candidates characteristically: a make few links and connections between literary texts, referring to superficial features b reflect views expressed in a limited way c assert a narrow range of meaning.	Candidates characteristically: a communicate a limited understanding of context through description of culture, text type, literary genre or historical period.
Band 2	Candidates characteristically: a communicate knowledge and some understanding of literary texts b present responses making use of appropriate terminology and examples to support interpretations c communicate content and meaning using straightforward language accurately d adopt a generalised approach.	Candidates characteristically: a identify some aspects of structure, form and language in literary texts b show awareness of writers' techniques, commenting on specific aspects with reference to how they shape meaning c make reference to texts to support their responses.	Candidates characteristically: a make links and connections between literary texts or note comparisons b communicate reasonable understanding of the views expressed in other interpretations or readings.	Candidates characteristically: a comment on some of the relationships between texts and their contexts b comment on how culture, text type, literary genre or historical period influence the reading of literary texts.
Band 3	Candidates characteristically: a communicate relevant knowledge and understanding of literary texts b present relevant responses using appropriate terminology and examples to support informed interpretations c structure and organise their increasingly coherent writing d communicate content and meaning through expressive and accurate writing.	Candidates characteristically: a identify relevant aspects of form, structure and language in literary texts b explore how writers use specific aspects to shape meaning c refer to relevant texts and sources to support their responses.	Candidates characteristically: a explore links and connections between literary texts in a systematic way b show clear understanding of views expressed in other interpretations or readings.	Candidates characteristically: a communicate understanding of relationships between specific literary texts and contexts b evaluate the influence of culture, text type, literary genre or historical period on the ways in which literary texts were written and were – and are – received.

	Candidates characteristically:	Candidates characteristically:	Candidates characteristically:	Candidates characteristically:
Band 4	**a** communicate detailed knowledge and understanding of literary texts **b** create and sustain well organised and coherent arguments, using appropriate terminology to support informed interpretations **c** structure and organise their writing using an appropriate critical register **d** communicate content and meaning through sophisticated, cogent and coherent writing.	**a** identify significant aspects of structure, form and language in literary texts **b** confidently explore through detailed and sophisticated critical analysis how writers use these aspects to create meaning **c** make detailed reference to texts and sources to support their responses.	**a** analyse and evaluate connections or points of comparison between literary texts **b** engage sensitively and with mature, informed understanding to different readings and interpretations.	**a** explore and analyse the significance of the relationships between specific literary texts and their contexts, making sophisticated comparisons **b** evaluate the influence of culture, text type, literary genre or historical period on the ways in which literary texts were written and were – and are – received.

Summary

In this introduction, we have considered:

- the choices you will be making

- the kinds of reading you will be doing

- the skills you need to develop

- the ways in which your work will be assessed.

No doubt you will want to revisit parts of this chapter and use it as a reference as you pursue your A2 studies.

We now turn to an exploration of the detail of the A2 course and begin in the next chapter with a consideration of the coursework in Unit 4.

2

Unit 4 coursework – the extended essay and Shakespeare study

The A2 coursework requirements

At AS you produced two pieces of coursework, one on a novel, and one on drama. The drama piece also asked you to make some links and comparisons **either** with the novel you had studied **or** with another play. You were able to refer to those texts as part of your wider reading when you answered the context question in the Unit 1 examination. You have therefore already learnt some of the skills needed to make comparisons between different texts, and also some ways of using your coursework texts as wider reading in an examination.

During your A2 year you will be expected to produce **one** coursework essay, of approximately **3,000 words**, comparing **three** whole texts: a Shakespeare play, and two others, which may be of any genre – prose, poetry or drama. As we said in Chapter 1, the aim of this A Level course is to enable you to develop into an informed and independent reader of, and writer about, all kinds of literary texts. For this reason, the examination board will not be giving you lists of books to choose from for this coursework essay, as it did for AS. With guidance from your teachers, your extended essay will give you the opportunity to make some real choices of which texts you read as part of your A Level course, and to write about the aspects of those texts that interest you.

In preparation for the A2 examination (Unit 3) you will be reading widely across time, looking at texts written by men and women, from the 14th century to the present day, and broadly linked by the theme of 'Love through the ages'. For your extended essay you have the choice of **either** linking your essay into the theme of love as well, **or** of deciding to concentrate on completely different elements in the texts you choose. The choice is up to you and your teacher.

The opportunities coursework offers you, as a reader and a writer

In the past, you may have seen coursework as something separate from your preparation for final examinations – something that you could 'get out of the way' so that you could concentrate on those. But A Level coursework is different: it is an essential part of your English Literature course where you can go on using all the skills that you have been practising at AS and which will also be assessed in your final examination paper. In your A2 extended essay you will be expected to show that you have developed all these skills more fully and can use them more independently:

- Reading skills: combining reading across texts, as well as reading closely to explore meanings and the ways writers express them.
- Planning skills: rereading, researching, note making, selecting textual evidence, and drafting.
- Writing skills: organising your ideas and producing a well thought out, accurately expressed and clearly argued piece of writing about texts.
- Editing skills (which combine reading and writing skills) – reading your own work critically, redrafting it to tighten up your argument and expression, and proofreading the final version thoroughly so that the final piece of work is the very best you can produce.

▓ Presentation skills:
  – making sure that you have quoted accurately, as in the original texts
  – compiling a bibliography (a list of references) which acknowledges any sources you have used
  – choosing an appropriate layout (line spacing, font, identification of titles of texts) which will make your work readable and conform to academic standards.

💡 The extended essay
⚡ Getting started and choosing your Shakespeare play

Shakespeare is bound to feature in your wider reading about love during your A2 year, and it is very likely that your teacher will make some of the plays the starting point for your extended essay as well. Not everybody in your group has to choose the same play. You still have an element of choice of which one to include in your essay. Think back over your past encounters with Shakespeare, and the plays you are familiar with. He wrote tragedies, such as *Othello*, and comedies like *Twelfth Night*, problem plays like *Measure for Measure*, plays about famous (and infamous) English kings – *Henry V* and *Richard III* – or about leadership and politics in Roman times – *Julius Caesar* and *Antony and Cleopatra*. Towards the end of his life, in plays like *The Winter's Tale* and *The Tempest*, his work became more philosophical. Which kind of play will you decide to work on?

💡 *Plays of William Shakespeare (1590–1616)*

It is not possible to be absolutely certain of the dates of composition of Shakespeare's plays. The timeline on p12 gives **approximate** dates of composition of the plays most frequently studied by students of English Literature in schools and colleges (less popular plays are included in brackets).

Because Shakespeare's plays are about human beings and their lives, no matter how distant or fantastic their settings in time and place may seem to be, these different kinds of play all contain variations on major themes, relating to the experience of being human, which run throughout literature:

▓ the whole range of relationships between men and women
▓ the experiences of women
▓ what it means to be a man
▓ relationships between parents and children
▓ tensions within families
▓ aspects of marriage
▓ facing old age
▓ attitudes towards death.

Shakespeare also dramatises big abstract ideas:

▓ the differences between appearances and realities (*Much Ado*, *Othello*)
▓ the workings of fate and chance (*Twelfth Night*, *Macbeth*)
▓ the effects of the past on the present (*The Winter's Tale*)
▓ the exercise of power (*The Taming of the Shrew*, *The Tempest*)
▓ concepts of good and evil, right and wrong, justice and morality (*Measure for Measure*, *The Merchant of Venice*)
▓ personal and political conflicts (*Antony and Cleopatra*, *Coriolanus*).

1564	Shakespeare born	
1590–91	(*Henry VI* Parts II and III)	(history)
1591–92	(*Henry VI* Part I)	(history)
1592–93	*Richard III*	history
	(*The Comedy of Errors*)	(comedy)
1593–94	*The Taming of the Shrew*	comedy
	(*Titus Andronicus*)	(tragedy)
1594–95	*Romeo and Juliet*	tragedy
	(*Two Gentlemen of Verona*)	(comedy)
	(*Love's Labours Lost*)	(comedy)
1595–96	*A Midsummer Night's Dream*	comedy
	Richard II	history
1596–97	*The Merchant of Venice*	comedy
	(*King John*)	(history)
1597–98	*Henry IV* Parts I and II	history
1598–99	*Much Ado About Nothing*	comedy
	Henry V	history
	(*The Merry Wives of Windsor*)	(comedy)
1599–1600	*Julius Caesar*	history
	As You Like It	comedy
1600–1	*Hamlet*	tragedy
1601–2	*Twelfth Night*	comedy
	(*Troilus and Cressida*)	(history)
1602–3	(*All's Well That Ends Well*)	(problem play)
1604–5	*Measure for Measure*	problem play
	Othello	tragedy
	King Lear	tragedy
1605–6	*Macbeth*	tragedy
1606–7	*Antony and Cleopatra*	history/tragedy
1607–8	*Coriolanus*	history
	(*Timon of Athens*)	(history)
1608–9	(*Pericles*)	(late play)
1609–10	(*Cymbeline*)	(late play)
1610–11	*The Winter's Tale*	late play
1611–12	*The Tempest*	late play
1616	Shakespeare dies	

In your chosen play you need to find a topic that you can then follow through into other texts, and on which you can base your comparison. This will mean reading the whole play, and establishing aspects of it that particularly interest you.

Before starting to choose more texts, it will help to write a short piece on the play you have chosen to work on, and the theme you are going to pursue – aim for about 1,000 words. This will give you a record of your thinking so far, and a draft which you can return to and rework to provide an early section of your whole essay. It will also be something which you can use, combined with references to the other two texts, as part of your introduction which establishes the basis of your comparisons which the rest of the essay is going to develop in more detail. Remember that you are not being asked to produce an essay that covers everything about Shakespeare's play, in all its complexity, but, having found your topic, to **select** from it the key ways in which Shakespeare presents your subject to the audience, and then **move outwards** from that starting point to make links with your two other texts.

For example, if you decide to work on *King Lear*, you might at first focus on parents and children, since the structure of the play with its main plot and subplot makes it clear this is a key theme. Your short piece on the play would identify the main episodes which involve parents and children, and help you to see that there is so much material that you need an even more precise focus on the play, in order to avoid producing a very generalised essay. If you then decide your subject will be relationships between fathers and sons, you would concentrate on Gloucester, Edmund and Edgar, but would not mention Lear himself. You might then choose Pip in *Great Expectations*, and consider his relationship with his two father figures, Joe and Magwitch. Finally, you could include a more modern text, like *I'm the King of the Castle* by Susan Hill, and consider what kind of a father Mr Hooper is to his son, compared with the three fathers you have considered so far. In dealing with each of the texts you would be concentrating on this particular aspect of each text, looking closely at the ways the writers present the fathers as individuals, comparing their characteristics, and linking these to the ways they treat their sons and how this affects their relationship with them.

Choosing two more texts

If you have taken advantage of the advice given you in the AS books to keep a personal Reading Log, you will already have some idea of the kinds of texts you enjoy reading and writing about to draw on. Remember that what you are supposed to be producing is a **literary** essay, which will show **through your comparison** that:

- you understand the content of both books well (AO1) and how they relate to the Shakespeare text (AO3)
- you can analyse the writers' different ways of presenting their subject matter and ideas (AO2)
- you have views of your own about the texts, and can consider and use other readers' views to help you develop these (AO3)
- you are aware of the usefulness to your interpretation of relevant contextual information (AO4).

Just choosing a book you read recently and really liked will not necessarily allow you to write a good comparative essay, however much you enjoyed reading it.

Ask yourself: What interested me most about this book?

- Was it just the story that kept the pages turning quickly, or was it the way the story was told?
- Was it just the situation – the terrible childhood of the writer or the main character, for example – or was it also the ways this was described?
- Was I just interested in the ideas in the book, or did I find the ways the writer put them across interesting as well?
- Can I think, on a first reading, of three or four different things I could say about the writer's techniques, their use of genres, point of view, their choices of language, for example?
- What does it have to say about the theme I have chosen for my essay?

Choosing good texts is really important. By 'good' texts, we mean texts whose subject matter provides you with real comparisons, not superficial ones, and texts that also give you plenty of opportunities to explore, comment on and compare the writers' styles and techniques, and how they present their ideas. Whether you choose to compare a Shakespeare play with a novel, another play or poetry, these techniques will include the writers' choices and uses of:

- genre
- narrative structures
- points of view: narrators, 'speakers' and 'voices' in texts
- ways of presenting characters (through description, dialogue etc.)
- ways of structuring the texts
- individual choices of language, and its effects
- the different ways writers develop similar themes.

Another crucial thing about choosing texts is to find the right partnerships – texts that have **similarities** (probably in their subject matter and themes) but also offer you plenty to say about the interesting **differences** between them in approaches to the subject, and in the ways they are written. Your wider reading for AS, and the ways you began to think about links between those texts, should help here, as well as the wider reading you are doing for 'Love through the ages', and the kinds of connections you are seeing between those texts.

Finding a focus

Once the Shakespeare play has been decided, you need a focus to organise your reading and ideas around. Rather general topics like the presentation of the main characters, or the central 'story', will probably be the first ideas you come up with, but you will write a much better essay if you have a strong focus on something more specific. So, as well as plot and characters, think about themes in the play, and aspects of writers' styles in any genre that could also make a good focus for comparison:

- different ways of telling similar stories
- creating characters, and using them – minor ones as well as main ones
- using settings
- creating atmosphere
- ways of directing the audience's or the reader's attention.

Having a Shakespeare play as one of your texts will probably mean that your other choices will be texts written in different genres, and possibly in different periods. This mixture will give you plenty of opportunities for comparisons of style as well as subject matter. For example, you could write:

- a comparison of the ways that Shakespeare, Jane Austen and Ian McEwan present aspects of marriage in *The Taming of the Shrew*, *Pride and Prejudice* and *On Chesil Beach*
- a comparison of the ways Shakespeare, Ibsen and Hisham Matar explore relationships between mothers and their sons in *Coriolanus*, *Ghosts* and *In the Country of Men*
- a comparison of the ways Shakespeare, Emily Brontë and Carol Anne Duffy explore kinds of love in *Romeo and Juliet*, *Wuthering Heights* and *Rapture*.

The ways the different writers handle a common theme are bound to be significantly different, depending on their choices of genre, their gender and the times at which they are writing. This will encourage you to pay attention to their choices of form, structure and language (AO2). It also makes it very relevant to consider how other readers, at the time of performance or publication as well as later, have reacted to these texts and ideas in comparison with your own response (AO3). These factors should also make you consider the contexts in which the texts were written, and what some information about these adds to your own interpretations of the texts you have chosen (AO4).

As well as choosing a mixture of periods and genres, either linked to the theme of love or independent of it, you could also choose:

- **three** plays by Shakespeare
- **one** Shakespeare play and **two other texts** written during the **same period**, for example, the ways Shakespeare and Webster present women in *King Lear*, the *Sonnets* and *The Duchess of Malfi*.

You also have the option of including **one non-fiction text**. Depending on your other two choices this could be any relevant non-fiction **prose** text, appropriate for a literary essay, including **contextual or cultural commentary**, or **literary criticism**, for example, a comparison of Shakespeare's presentation of Hero and Lady Macbeth, and an analysis of Shakespeare's dramatic techniques, in *Much Ado About Nothing*, *Macbeth* and *Clamorous Voices: Shakespeare's women today* (Carol Rutter, 1988).

Clamorous Voices is a collection of personal commentaries by five well-known contemporary women actors on some major female roles in Shakespeare's plays. In 'Lady Macbeth's barren sceptre', Sinead Cusack talks about her interpretation of Lady Macbeth, and how she arrived at it. For an essay like this, you would need to treat her commentary as a text in its own right, looking at Cusack's ideas about Lady Macbeth's character, and how she develops these ideas.

You might start from your own impressions of Hero and Lady Macbeth, and any similarities you can find in their situations or in Shakespeare's presentation of them, and then move to a closer examination of Cusack's piece, using it to explore what strikes you about her interpretation, and the ways it enhances your understanding of Shakespeare's dramatic techniques. This could then take you back to look more closely at Hero, perhaps by imagining the process an actor would have to go through to bring her to life as a character, and you could finish by offering your own fuller reading of her part and her contribution to the play.

Preparing to write the essay

Deciding on your texts and a working title is a major step towards producing your extended essay. Your teachers will have to show these to your Centre's moderator for their approval during the autumn term, and will get feedback from them, which will be helpful to you. The moderator sees ideas and work from many different schools and colleges and can offer useful advice, but this can only be helpful to you if you get it before you have put a lot of effort into writing the essay. Once you have chosen your texts and possible title, write a short statement of what you intend to cover in the essay to add to your piece on the Shakespeare play, noting down 3–5 main areas of the texts you plan to cover in your comparison. This will be useful to you as a skeleton plan, and will let your teacher see how you are going to tackle your coursework essay.

While you are **rereading** your chosen texts, **keep systematic notes** of:

▨ references to the texts that you think you are going to want to make – key scenes relevant to your topic, and useful quotations, with clear page references

▨ sources of any secondary materials you use, with full details of texts read or internet sites visited.

While you are developing your own interpretations of the texts:

▨ do some research into what some other readers have thought about your books, to help you to clarify, confirm or perhaps alter your initial reactions and ideas

▨ check out details of when the texts were written, and find out more about the contexts in which they were produced, which may affect your views about them.

All this will take time, so make sure that your teacher gives you a clear timescale to work to.

Writing the essay: drafting and re-drafting

There is every temptation in the world to put off getting down to writing what feels like a huge essay. Being given a set time at which you will be expected to make a start will be very helpful to you, and your teacher may set aside some class time when you will write your first draft. By that time you should have an idea of what you want to say about the books, and you will have your notes with you. Sort these out in advance, and when the time comes, write.

Don't agonise about your first paragraph – many writers leave their opening paragraphs to the last, anyway, so just get going. You won't know what you really think until you see what you have to say! Once you have a draft, you have the makings of the essay which you can work on, pulling and pushing your points into the right order, adding in references and details, and sharpening up your own style. You will have to have completed a final version by the end of the spring term and all this takes time – allow for it. Allow also for leaving the essay alone for a few weeks, so that you come back to it to complete the final draft and read it as a critic, rather than as a stressed author.

To summarise

To produce a successful final piece of coursework, you are going to have to do the following:

▨ **Choose** your three texts wisely.

▨ Read them to find the relevant material for your comparison.

- **Reread** the texts, picking out similarities and significant differences, and the ways the writers present them.
- **Make notes** on these similarities and differences, identifying useful references and quotations.
- Do some **research** into some **other readers' views** about the texts, and about their **contexts**.
- Produce a **first draft**.
- **Revise** your draft in the light of comments from your teacher.
- Produce a **second**, **final draft**, paying *attention* to the **structure and presentation of your ideas**. For example, look at the ways your opening sentences introduce each paragraph, and link with what has gone before, your integration of textual references, your management of links and comparisons between texts, and the accuracy of your spelling and punctuation.
- Be prepared to **edit** your final draft if necessary. You may have gone well over (or under) the suggested word limit of 3,000 words, or your opening and/or closing paragraphs may need revising and sharpening up.
- **Proofread** your final version carefully. Then leave time to put it on one side for a few days, so that you can give it a final objective reading before you hand it in.

Assessment

Your A2 coursework is worth 40% of your final marks. It will be assessed first by your teachers, using the criteria and Assessment Grid. Their assessment will then be checked by your moderator. Moderators enjoy seeing the final piece of work they have been involved in developing, so you can be sure that you have a real audience beyond your teacher for what you have written.

Link

The Assessment Grid is printed at the end of Chapter 1.

Summary

Keys to success

As well as good choices of texts, and well-focused titles, success in your coursework will depend on:

- well-planned use of time to make the best use of the opportunities coursework offers
- a title that focuses on writers' styles as well as on subject matter
- comparisons that move between all three texts
- sustained focus on writers' choices of form, structure and language
- well-selected references to the texts
- brief, well-chosen quotations, used as part of fully developed points
- a clear line of argument
- evidence of personal interest in, and independent thinking about, the texts
- thoughtful use of other readers' interpretations
- awareness of the relevance of contextual information, and its contribution to your understanding of your chosen texts and topic
- a carefully edited and proofread final essay.

Introduction

In the second chapter of this book we looked at how to approach the coursework unit. For the rest of the book we will deal in some detail with your preparation for the examination. The two units could be linked through the theme of love, but that is a choice which rests with you and your teachers. So our focus is now on Unit 3.

This chapter will set the scene and show you how to plan your reading and study. Then the following three chapters will each, in turn, cover one of the main genres – **poetry**, **prose** and **drama** – introducing you to the kinds of reading, detailed study and recording you need to do. Each of these three chapters will look at the **growth** and **development** of each genre through **time**, inviting you to study some texts or extracts closely and suggesting appropriate **wider reading**. The final chapter will show you how all this reading comes to be applied to the Unit 3 examination by presenting you with a specimen paper.

The examination paper

The extracts and the questions

The paper will consist of **two compulsory questions** on four unprepared texts, covering all three genres. All four texts/extracts on the paper will be on the subject of **love**, and will be further connected through a theme such as 'partings' or 'loss'.

The first question will present you with two texts of the same genre. If you turn to Chapter 7 you will see that the first question on the specimen paper refers to two sonnets. The genre chosen for the first question may be any of the three genres.

The second question will refer to two texts from the other two genres. In the specimen paper the two extracts in this question are taken from a novel and a play.

The first question will ask you to compare the two texts in some detail, and, where appropriate, to refer to your wider reading. The second question will ask you to compare the two texts and will specifically require you to compare them with your wider reading across the literature of love.

Preparing for the unprepared

As the final examination paper consists of unprepared extracts and texts, it is essential that you approach the paper with the relevant knowledge and understanding as well as the confidence to 'place' the extracts in context and to analyse them. Tackling the unprepared extracts requires high-order skills appropriate to the end of an A Level course. All your experience of wide and close reading as well as of developing and supporting an interpretation will come into play. Remember what we said in Chapter 1 about there being no 'right answers'. No 'learned notes' or teacher interpretation can help you here – you have become the **autonomous reader** and have sole responsibility in this paper for making meaning from the texts. **The extracts are unprepared, but you must not be!**

Link

To see examples of these extracts and questions in a specimen examination paper, turn to Chapter 7.

Your preparation must consist of:

- relevant and appropriate **wide reading** across time, genre and gender
- continuous **practice** in tackling unseen texts.

Assessment

All four Assessment Objectives are tested by the two questions. You have already seen in Chapter 1 the general A2 marking grid based on these four Assessment Objectives. If you turn to Chapter 7, you will see how the general grid translates into specific assessment grids for each question.

▪ Your preparation

We now turn to consider what you need to **do, know and understand** in order to have maximum success in the examination.

Making choices

A key factor in your preparation is your development as reader and critic, taking increasing responsibility for selection of your wider reading. The whole of English Literature is at your disposal and it is important that you move from a course guided by **teacher choice** to a situation where you develop **autonomy** as a reader. This course gives you every opportunity for such development since there are **no set texts** and you have a great deal of freedom in making choices.

Kinds of reading

As well as your work in the classroom with your teacher, you need to make time for **regular private reading** so that you are better equipped to compare, evaluate and interpret texts. Sharing your reading experiences and your insights with your peers will give you practice in expressing your insights as you learn to support your opinions; it will also provide opportunities to take other readers' opinions into account.

The composition of your reading should be a mixture of **whole** texts and **extracts**. Reading extracts enables you to cover a wider range of genres and times, and, in its turn, will no doubt encourage you to read more whole texts!

Remember that the act of reading is not always the same. You are preparing for a paper where you will read unprepared texts **closely** in order to analyse and make meaning, and you will certainly be doing a good deal of **close** reading, using the tools and questions for analysis that we offered you in Chapter 1. At other times you will read for gist, or to trace immediate connections of theme or attitude as you build your **wide reading portfolio**.

Our expectation of you as a wide reader is that you will not only read a great number of texts in the **canon** but that you will also read outside the core classic texts. There is of course debate about the canon. The traditional view is that a list of core classics, with intrinsic literary value, provides us with a common shared area of experience and informs us about our cultural history. Other critics claim that the canon is too narrow and imposes a restricting conformity, maintaining that the canon is largely made up of works by white, male and dead authors and that it discriminates against women. Our approach is to encourage you not only to read works from the canon in order to understand and explore literary tradition, but also to challenge its boundaries and read contemporary writing, works by female writers and post-colonial texts.

🔍 The literature of love

All your reading for this unit will relate to the central theme of *Love through the ages*. For the purposes of this examination, we define *love* as **human love** (not love of God or love of a pet). No doubt the majority of your reading will be on the subject of **romantic love**. The following poem, written by Lord Byron to a young man, is an example of such a love poem:

Poem A

Stanzas for Music

There be none of Beauty's daughters
With a magic like thee;
And like music on the waters
Is thy sweet voice to me:
When, as if its sound were causing
The charmed ocean's pausing,
The waves lie still and gleaming,
And the lull'd winds seem dreaming:
And the midnight moon is weaving
Her bright chain o'er the deep;
Whose breast is gently heaving,
As an infant's asleep:
So the spirit bows before thee,
To listen and adore thee;
With a full but soft emotion,
Like the swell of Summer's ocean.

Lord Byron

Fig. 3.1 *Lord Byron*

But you may also wish to explore writing on other close, intimate and loving relationships such as those in the following two poems – the mother and child in the Plath poem and the friends in the Jennings poem.

Poem B

Friends

I fear it's very wrong of me
And yet I must admit it,
When someone offers friendship
I want the whole of it.
I don't want everybody else
To share my friends with me.
At least, I want one special one,
Who, indisputably,

Likes me much more than all the rest,
Who's always on my side,
Who never cares what others say,
Who lets me come and hide
Within his shadow, in his house –
It doesn't matter where –
Who lets me simply be myself,
Who's always, always there.

Elizabeth Jennings

Poem C

Morning Song

Love set you going like a fat gold watch,
The midwife slapped your footsoles, and your bald cry
Took its place among the elements.

Our voices echo, magnifying your arrival. New statue.
In a drafty museum, your nakedness
Shadows our safety. We stand round blankly as walls.

I'm no more your mother
Than the cloud that distils a mirror to reflect its own slow
Effacement at the wind's hand.

All night your moth-breath
Flickers among the flat pink roses. I wake to listen:
A far sea moves in my ear.

One cry, and I stumble from bed, cow-heavy and floral
In my Victorian nightgown.
Your mouth opens clean as a cat's. The window square

Whitens and swallows its dull stars. And now you try
Your handful of notes;
The clear vowels rise like balloons.

Sylvia Plath

Fig. 3.2 Mother and Child *by Pablo Picasso*

i Activity

1 Study each of these poems closely by applying the template of questions presented in Chapter 1 (see close readings, pp5–6). You may wish to share your findings with other members of your class.

2 Start your wider reading, by reaching out from each of the poems and by finding other poems on:

- romantic love
- love of friends
- maternal love.

3 Then move on to find representations of these kinds of love in the other genres. This way of working (reading texts closely and then linking them to the rest of your reading) should by now be familiar to you after the completion of your AS course.

Developing an overview of English Literature

The combination of **close** and **wide** reading that made up your AS studies will need to be strengthened, widened and deepened in this second year of the course. At AS, all your texts were part of a 'shared context' – whether it was **Victorian**, **World War One**, or **Twentieth Century**. Here, in the final year of the course, your reading forms a coherent collection of texts from the whole of English Literature, linked by theme, spanning time and tradition, genres and gender. As well as a close and in-depth knowledge of individual texts, you need to have an **overview of the development of literature through the ages** and of the **influences on writers, texts and readers**. The following activity, based on extracts of different genres and taken from different times, introduces you to a way of working that you will need to adopt as you:

- link your texts through theme
- practise close analysis of text
- explore similarities and differences
- place your texts in context
- explore ways of interpreting texts.

Q Activity

Here are three extracts, one from each genre taken from different times and raditions of writing: the first is from the 17th-century play *Antony and Cleopatra* by William Shakespeare; the second from the 19th-century novel *Wuthering Heights* by Emily Brontë; and the third is a poem by the 20th-century poet W.H. Auden. The speaker in each piece is describing a male romantic hero with whom s/he is in love.

Read the three extracts carefully, then consider:

- how each extract portrays the romantic hero
- the writer's choices of form, structure and language
- the influence of the time of writing on each extract
- the similarities and differences between the three extracts in both subject matter and style.

Extract D

From *Antony and Cleopatra*

Cleopatra: Noblest of men, woo't die?
Hast thou no care of me? Shall I abide
In this dull world, which in thy absence is
No better than a sty?
(Antony dies)
O see, my women,
The crown o'th' earth doth melt. My lord!
O, withered is the garland of the war.
The soldier's pole is fall'n. Young boys and girls
Are level now with men. The odds is gone,
And there is nothing left remarkable
Beneath the visiting moon.

William Shakespeare

Fig. 3.3 *Still from a production of* **Antony and Cleopatra**

Extract E

From *Wuthering Heights*

I cannot express it; but surely you and everybody have a notion
that there is, or should be an existence of yours beyond you. What
were the use of my creation, if I were entirely contained here? My
great miseries in this world have been Heathcliff's miseries, and
I watched and felt each from the beginning; my great thought in
living is himself. If all else perished, and he remained, I should still
continue to be; and if all else remained, and he were annihilated,
the universe would turn to a mighty stranger. I should not seem a
part of it. My love for Linton is like the foliage in the woods; time
will change it, I'm well aware, as winter changes the trees. My love
for Heathcliff resembles the eternal rocks beneath: a source of little
visible delight, but necessary. Nelly, I am Heathcliff! He's always,
always in my mind: not as a pleasure to myself, but as my own
being. So don't talk of our separation again – it is impracticable; ...

Emily Brontë

Extract F

Stop all the clocks, cut off the telephone

Stop all the clocks, cut off the telephone,
Prevent the dog from barking with a juicy bone,
Silence the pianos and with muffled drum
Bring out the coffin, let the mourners come.

Let aeroplanes circle moaning overhead
Scribbling on the sky the message He is Dead,
Put crepe bows round the white necks of the public doves,
Let the traffic policeman wear black cotton gloves.

He was my North, my South, my East and West,
My working week and my Sunday rest,
My noon, my midnight, my talk, my song;
I thought that love would last for ever: I was wrong.

The stars are not wanted now: put out every one;
Pack up the moon and dismantle the sun;
Pour away the ocean and sweep up the wood;
For nothing now can ever come to any good.

W.H. Auden

When you are an established reader in the literature of love, you will be able to go on to make connections between these three texts and your wider reading.

Your reading for the course should start with Chaucer and progress through time until you reach contemporary writing. You need to be familiar with the ways in which social, historical and cultural contexts shape the literary tradition, and with how your texts reflect or challenge the contexts in which they are written.

As part of your wider reading, you should conduct **research into contexts**. Always find out about the writer of the text, and, if you can, the time when it was written and published. Oxford and Cambridge University Presses both publish a *Companion to English Literature* for biographical and historical facts, and you might find it useful to refer to *The Concise Oxford Chronology of English Literature*; references within a text will suggest areas where you need further investigation, and skimming critical works or contemporary and later reviews can provide interpretations by other readers.

💡 As you develop an overview, you will notice that each period is of course influenced by the preceding one, either reacting against or continuing to develop it. Like all artistic movements, literature tends to swing in reaction against the previous age. As you read more and more widely, you will develop a feel for each period, its ideas and ways of expressing them. Through research and wide reading, you will gain insights into, knowledge about and understanding of the key periods:

- Medieval
- Elizabethan and Jacobean
- Restoration
- Augustan

▨ Romantic

▨ Victorian and Edwardian

▨ Modernist

▨ Post-modernist

– and you can record your findings in your Reading Log.

💡 *Literature through time grid*

To get you started, we have designed the **English Literature through time grid** which you will find on pp124–5 of this book. It brings together information about periods/movements, writers, social and literary contexts as well as critical theories through time. The grid provides you with a **starting point**; your own reading and research will fill in necessary detail so that you can effectively analyse the ways a text reflects and/or challenges its context.

Interesting areas for research, exploration and questioning might be:

🔢 the Medieval and Elizabethan **world picture** (see *The Elizabethan World Picture* by E.M.W. Tillyard)

▨ how and why **changes** to this world picture affected literature through the centuries

▨ the impact of accelerated **social change** in the 20th century on literature

▨ the emergence or dominance of a particular **genre** at a particular time – the next three chapters will look at this in some detail; for example, you will see that drama is the oldest genre, and that the 18th century saw the emergence of the novel as a new genre

▨ the balance/imbalance of male and female writing during a particular era – you will notice that for much of the history of English Literature, **male** writers are dominant.

You will notice that the grid has a column for critical theory. We consider it useful for you to be familiar with different approaches to textual analysis, but our view is that a detailed study of literary critical theory is more appropriate to a university undergraduate degree course. We have already established that texts are capable of multiple meanings and may be viewed differently by different readers. We recommend that you, the reader, acknowledge and embrace different views and critical positions rather than limit yourself to a single interpretation or slavish following of one critical theory. Developing awareness of different ways of reading and possible different interpretations is a crucial part of your development as an **informed autonomous reader and critic**. The main critical theories are listed chronologically on the **English Literature through time grid**. Your task is to research what the labels mean and to come to a basic understanding of the various critical positions.

Further reading

A good place to begin your research would be to read:

▪ *Beginning Theory* by Peter Barry (Manchester University Press)

▪ *Text, Reader, Critic* in the EMC Advanced Literature Series (The English and Media Centre)

Summary

In order to succeed in this paper, you need to develop:

■ an overview of the development of literature through the ages

■ an understanding of the contextual influences on writers and texts

■ an appreciation of the ways in which texts may be interpreted by different readers.

Poetry about love

- introduces wider reading of poetry about love from Chaucer to the present day in poems by men and women

- develops awareness of the importance of writers' choices of form, structure and language in the writing and reading of poetry, and the development of the genre across time

- provides examples for further study of subject matter and styles, making links and connections between texts

- shows how the Assessment Objectives can be applied to your reading.

Link

You will find the English Literature through time grid on pp124–5 of this book.

Link

To remind yourself of the questions presented in Chapter 1, see pp5–6.

Link

For more information on the wider reading portfolio, see Chapter 1, pp6–7.

Introduction

At AS your work on poetry laid the foundations for further study of the genre. You were reading within the boundaries of a defined length of time, but within that, whichever of the three options you studied, you could see from your wider reading the different ways in which writers of the period approached shared subject matter, and the similarities and differences in their styles. At A2 you will be expected to extend this across time, from the 14th century (and before) to the present day, still reading texts from all three genres (poetry, prose and drama) by women as well as men.

Your reading log

Throughout your work in this chapter you will need to keep a log of the poetry texts you have come across. Whether you use the online resources, or a paper file, such record keeping is vital as it will become your revision tool for the examination. This chapter does not cover the rich and vast range of poetry texts available to you, but will cover many of the popular forms and styles throughout time. You need to remember to keep your **reading log**, recording both **genre** and **time**, making sure to include cross-references between poems, and connections with extracts from drama and prose.

As you study the poems that follow, we have provided questions to help you, but for a fuller analytical study of an extract or whole poem remember to use the questions we gave you in Chapter 1.

Don't forget to also keep your **wider reading portfolio** up to date.

Investigating poets' choices

Subject matter

Poetry is the genre most obviously associated with the literature of love. Open any general anthology of poetry and, regardless of period, you will find poems exploring every aspect of love and human relationships:

- romantic love – between boys and girls, men and women, men and men, women and women

- married love

- love between parents and children

- love between siblings.

Also, across time, you will find poems about:

- falling in love

- love at first sight

- true love

- unrequited love

- secret love

- obsession

- jealousy

- ▇ betrayal
- ▇ loss and grief
- ▇ love after death.

As you work through this chapter and the poems in it, the activities will increasingly be asking you to link and compare poems, in terms of their subjects, the poets' attitudes to love, and their different styles. Classifying poems under headings like the ones above will help you to read more closely, and to develop a critical vocabulary of your own which can describe, analyse and interpret shades of meaning and variations in tone.

Because of the universality of the theme, you are bound to find links with some of the poetry (and the prose and drama) which you read at GCSE and AS. One way to start on your wider reading in the literature of love could be to revisit the poems you think are most relevant, and reread them to find examples of some of these kinds of love to start from.

▇ Reading and making meaning: form and structure

◍ Form

Readers sometimes find it hard to see the difference between the **form** and the **structure** of a text when reading and trying to understand it. Think of the **form** of a text as a box – and of all the different materials and shapes and sizes boxes can come in. Form is closely related to genre, and writers' choices of forms are influenced by the time at which they are writing (their literary and historical context), and to a certain extent by what is 'in fashion' in poetry, prose or drama at the time.

As far as poetry is concerned, whatever the subject matter, a poet has a huge choice of possible forms to choose from. The major ones which this chapter will be referring to are:

- ▇ **ballad**
- ▇ **ode**
- ▇ **sonnet**
- ▇ **lyric**
- ▇ **couplet**
- ▇ **blank verse**
- ▇ **free verse**.

All poetic forms traditionally have a set of distinctive rules, or conventions, for a poet to follow. These may be about **stanza** length, or rhyme schemes, or metre, or numbers of syllables in a line. Readers who don't write poetry themselves tend to think that these rules must inevitably restrict the writer's ability to express him or herself, but poets who choose to work within the constraints of a given form do so because they enjoy the technical challenge and the discipline. **Form** provides a set of labels that run across time, so that you will find poets in the 20th and 21st centuries writing sonnets, lyrics or blank verse just as often as earlier poets did, and observing a similar set of basic rules. As you read through the ages you will be able to see the ways different forms are used creatively, as writers in later periods revisit earlier ones, bending and breaking the rules, not just obeying them.

The relation of rhyme and metre to form

Rhyme is one element of most poetic forms. It can be part of the patterns of words and sounds a poet sets up in the poem and can affect pace and tone to a certain extent, but it contributes nothing to the meaning of a poem on its own. Meaning depends on the poet's decisions about structure and choices of language and vocabulary. So cataloguing rhyme schemes is not useful – but being alert to different kinds of rhyme can be. As well as end rhymes, which are easy to spot, pararhyme, or masculine and feminine rhymes and their effects, or half rhymes, all contribute to different effects in poems, but always in combination with the poet's words.

The **metre** you are probably most familiar with is the **iambic pentameter**. It is the basis of Shakespeare's blank verse – the 10 syllable, 5 beat line said to be the natural **rhythm** of English speech, or the human heartbeat. There are many other metres that poets can use, and for them to opt for a particular metre does not mean that they are limiting their powers of expression. You only need to look at how Shakespeare manipulates the rhythms of his blank verse to achieve lifelike speech and emotions in *Twelfth Night* or *Othello*, and then sample a few lines of Milton's *Paradise Lost* or Wordsworth's *Prelude* to see and hear how versatile the metre of blank verse can be.

Structure

If you accept the idea of form as the big box, then the structure of the poem is the way a poet packs the subject matter into the box – form is the external organisation of the poem, structure is its internal organisation: the ways the poet develops the subject from the beginning to the end. Concentrating on:

- what the poem seems to be about
- how the sentences and the verses are connected
- how the poet brings the poem to a conclusion

will get you much further into understanding a poem than any amount of checking rhyme schemes, beating out the metre or spotting examples of poetic devices like **assonance** and alliteration without relating them to meaning.

Fig. 4.1 The Painter's Honeymoon *by Frederick, Lord Leighton (1830–96)*

Exploring the interaction of form, structure and language

To make meaning of a poem most effectively you should:

- read in units of sense, not line by line (use the punctuation to help you)
- be aware of sentence lengths and consider sentence types: questions, exclamations or statements, and the effects of these within the poem
- notice turning points within poems, and shifts within, or between, stanzas – these may be in tenses, or in ideas
- look for patterns in the language: repetitions and contrasts
- watch out for unfamiliar vocabulary and word order.

When a poet decides to write in a particular form, especially one that involves a strict rhyme scheme, this will have an impact on his or her choices of vocabulary, and also on the order in which words are arranged within a line, a sentence or a stanza. Sometimes this can make the meaning difficult to understand at first, but once you are aware of the need to pay attention to word order, you will be able to read the lines more flexibly, and their meaning will become much clearer. Being conscious of unusual word order will also draw your attention to patterns of language within the poem, and help you to explore its structure more thoroughly.

As an example, look at the first four lines of Shakespeare's *Sonnet 42*:

> That thou hast her, it is not all my grief,
> And yet it may be said I loved her dearly;
> That she hath thee is of my wailing chief,
> A loss in love that touches me more nearly.

If this idea about losing the beloved to a rival were written in prose the words would certainly be in quite a different order. Shakespeare uses the form of his sonnet's first quatrain, with its a-b-a-b rhyme scheme, to explore 'ownership' in love. He places the idea of 'who possesses who' at the beginning of lines 1 and 3 and keeps the end of the first three lines for the phrases that emphasise his sense of loss, linking them together, obviously through meaning but also by rhyme. He then sums up that section of the poem with a straightforward statement of his feeling, clinching it with the final rhyme.

Texts and traditions: the literary context

Poetry about love has a long history. From Chaucer's day to the early 20th century, educated people would read classical literature – Homer's *Iliad* and *Odyssey*, Virgil's *Aeneid* and his pastoral poetry, and love poetry by Horace and Catullus – and they would know the myths and legends of the ancient gods and goddesses from Ovid's *Metamorphoses*. Renaissance writers and readers also knew the poetry of France and Italy, especially the love poems of Petrarch and the stories of Boccacio, and found in them ideas and models to use in their own work.

All authors write with some knowledge of what has been done before them in their chosen genre; at the same time, they are writing within their contemporary context. The poets you are going to read all show their awareness of poetic conventions but also adapt, and often subvert, these by the ways they use form, structure and language to express individual thoughts and feelings. Modern readers have inevitably lost a great deal of what was once a shared context of reading and shared frames of reference, but we can still see the traditions persisting across time as writers constantly revisit themes and forms. Recognising aspects of their literary context will enrich your own reading of poems from earlier centuries.

📕 Gender in the poetry of love

Much of the earliest love poetry in chronologically organised anthologies is attributed to Anonymous. Some critics have suggested that this conceals the identity of a female poet. It is an interesting idea, and although internal evidence will often make it obvious that the poem is written from a male point of view, just ask yourself what difference it could make to your interpretation of the tone and meanings of these two short poems, if you read them as written by a woman, rather than making the usual assumption that the voice in them is a man's.

Plucking the rushes: a boy and girl are sent to gather rushes for thatching.

Green rushes with red shoots,
Long leaves bending to the wind –
You and I in the same boat
Plucking rushes at the Five Lakes.

We started at dawn from the orchid-island:
We rested under elms till noon.
You and I plucking rushes
Had not plucked a handful when night came!

Chinese, 4th century translated by Arthur Waley

O Western wind, when wilt thou blow
    That the small rain down can rain?
Christ, that my love were in my arms,
    And I in my bed again!

Anon, about 1500

In poetry about love you will be aware of the dominance of male voices, male attitudes to love and sex, and of women being the constant subject of the male gaze. Poetry by women is rarely found in anthologies until well into the 20th century. This is largely a result of the politics of publishing. Male editors select texts from the (predominantly male) canon – as you will see if you skim through the contents of F.T. Palgrave's *The Golden Treasury* (1861) or the first edition of Sir Arthur Quiller Couch's *Oxford Book of English Verse* (1900). From the early 19th century onwards increasing numbers of poems by women were being published, and by the end of the 20th century, largely thanks to the combination of feminist thinking and publishers willing to publish their work, poetry by women is as available to readers as poetry by men.

Link

To remind yourself of how to compile and use your **wider reading portfolio**, see Chapter 1, pp6–7.

Activity

Consider the difficulties of achieving a balance of gender in your wider reading of the poetry of love.

- Why is this so?
- Think about how male writers present women in their poems, and give them a voice and presence, even if they deny them the right of reply.

Use the results of your thoughts to help you as you compile your own collection of love poetry in your wider reading portfolio.

Love poetry through the ages

The ballad

At the end of the 17th century, the novelist Sir Walter Scott began to collect ballads and publish them in his *Minstrelsy of the Scottish Border*. The ballad has been a popular form with poets and writers of song lyrics ever since. The reason for starting this chronological survey of love poetry with ballads is because, although it is very difficult to give them precise dates of composition, they were originally an oral form of poetry. A typical ballad is a mixture of storytelling and speech rather than writing. Its popular themes are love and the supernatural, often woven together in the narrative of some dramatic event. The poetic form is simple – usually a four-line stanza – which tells the story clearly and directly, often in dialect. Dialogue, rhyme, repetition or a refrain is used to make the verse more accessible and memorable.

Helen of Kirconnell (or Fair Helen)

I wish I were where Helen lies,
Night and day on me she cries;
O that I were where Helen lies
   On fair Kirconnell lea!

Curst be the heart that thought the thought,
And curst the hand that fired the shot,
When in my arms burd Helen dropt,
   And died to succour me!

O think na ye my heart was sair,
When my Love dropt down and spake nae mair!
I laid her down wi' meikle care
   On fair Kirconnell lea.

As I went down the water-side,
None but my foe to be my guide,
None but my foe to be my guide
   On fair Kirconnell lea;

I lighted down my sword to draw,
I hacked him in pieces sma'
I hacked him in pieces sma'
   For her sake that died for me.

O Helen fair, beyond compare!
I'll make a garland o' thy hair
Shall bind my heart for evermair
   Until the day I dee!

O that I were where Helen lies!
Night and day on me she cries;
Out of my bed she bids me rise,
   Says, 'Haste, and come to me!'

O Helen fair! O Helen chaste!
If I were with thee I were blest,
Where thou lies low and takes thy rest,
   On fair Kirconnell lea.

I wish my grave were growing green,
A winding-sheet drawn ower my een,
And I in Helen's arms lying,
   On fair Kirconnell lea.

I wish I were where Helen lies!
Night and day on me she cries;
And I am weary of the skies,
   Since my Love died for me.

Anon

Fig. 4.2 Paolo and Francesca *by Charles Edward Halle (1846–1919)*

Further reading

Traditional ballads (try searching for these on the internet):

- *Childe Maurice*
- *The Wife of Usher's Well*
- *Lord Randal*
- *Barbara Allen*
- *Tam Lin*
- *True Thomas / Thomas the Rhymer*

Using the ballad form:

- *Cold is the Earth* by Emily Brontë
- *The Rime of the Ancient Mariner* by Samuel Taylor Coleridge
- *La Belle Dame sans Merci* by John Keats
- * *As I Walked Out One Evening* by W.H. Auden
- * *Ballad of the Bread Man* by Charles Causley
- * *Timothy Winters* by Charles Causley
- * *The Shooting of Dan McGrew* by Robert Service
- * *The Ballad of Rudolph Reed* by Gwendolyn Brooks

* in *The Rattle Bag*, eds Seamus Heaney & Ted Hughes (Faber)

Questions

AO1: Developing an **informed response** to the text
- Describe what happens in the poem.
- What are the thoughts and feelings presented in it?

AO2: Understanding how structure, form and language shape meaning
- What do you notice about the ways the writer uses form, structure and language in this ballad to tell the story?

AO3: Exploring connections, comparisons and the interpretations of other readers
- Compare this ballad with others of a similar period, or with a modern lyric or folk song.
- How do you respond to the view that a ballad can only tell a simple story because its form and language are so simple?

AO4: Understanding of the significance and influence of contexts
- What features of this ballad can help you to establish some sort of historical or cultural context for it?

The Middle Ages: the 14th century

Geoffrey Chaucer

Geoffrey Chaucer (1342–1400) is a major figure in English literature. Professionally he was a courtier, a diplomat and a civil servant during the reigns of Edward III and Richard II. He travelled widely in Europe as a young man, read French and Italian texts, and was the first poet to show that English was just as appropriate a language for poetry as French or Latin. His best-known work is *The Canterbury Tales*. Many of the stories told by Chaucer's pilgrims on their way to the shrine of St Thomas à Becket at Canterbury deal with love, sometimes tragically, sometimes comically and sometimes to deliver a moral message. Chaucer includes two women among his storytellers: the Prioress and the garrulous Wife of Bath, who gives the other pilgrims the benefit of her views on love and marriage in her Prologue, before telling her story, which answers the question 'What thyng is it that wommen moost desiren? ('What do women really want?').

The answer is:

> Wommen desiren to have sovereynetee
> As wel over hir housbond as hir love,
> And for to been in maistrie hym above.

(In other words, power over their husbands!)

In the following extracts from *The Miller's Tale*, Chaucer presents the competing lovers of Alisoun, an old carpenter's young and sexy wife. The story is set in Oxford, and the first extract is preceded by the Miller's detailed description of Alisoun's many physical attractions. Not surprisingly, Nicholas, the university student who is lodging in the carpenter's house, can't resist her.

Using your own knowledge of chat-up lines, and the ways people behave in this sort of situation, see how much of Chaucer's racy narrative you can understand.

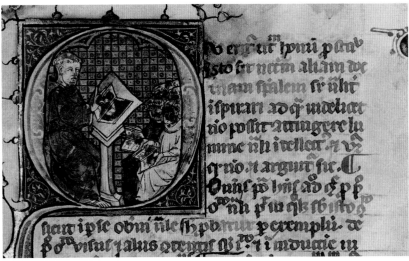

Fig. 4.3 *Part of a medieval manuscript*

So bifel the case
That on a day this hende Nicholas
Fil with this yonge wyf to <u>rage</u> and pleye,
Whil that hir housbonde was at Oseneye,
As clerkes ben ful subtile and ful <u>queynte</u>;
And prively he caughte hir by the <u>queynte</u>,
And sayde, 'Ywis, but if ich have my wille,
For deerne love of thee, lemman, I spille.'
And heeld hire harde by the haunche-bones,
And said, '<u>Lemman</u>, love me al atones,
Or I will dyen, also God me save!'
And she sproong as a colt dooth in the <u>trave</u>
And with hir heed she wryeth fast awey,
And seyde, 'I wol nat kisse thee, by my fey!
Why, lat be,' quod she, 'lat be, Nicholas,
Or I wol cry 'out harrow' and 'allas'!
Do wey youre handes, for youre curteisye!'
    This Nicholas gan mercy for to crye,
And spak so fair, and profred him so faste,
That she hir love hym graunted atte laste,
And swoor hir ooth, by seint Thomas of Kent,
That she wol been at his comandement,
Whan that she may hir <u>leyser</u> wel espie.
'Myn housbonde is so ful of jalousie
That but ye wayte wel and been privee,
I woot right wel I nam but deed' quod she.

The Miller's Tale, lines 3268–3296

> ### Modern language
>
> **rage:** flirt
>
> **queynte:** 1. cunning
>   2. female genitalia
>
> **lemman:** sweetheart
>
> **trave:** a wooden frame to keep a
> horse still
>
> **leyser:** leisure, chance

Alisoun's other admirer is Absolon, the parish clerk, much the same age as Nicholas, but a very different sort of lover. Poets writing about love during the Middle Ages were influenced by the ideals of **courtly love**. The literary convention of this kind of love is that the lady is seen as the object of male worship, rather than of sexual desire, and the lover presents himself as her servant. In this extract he tries to attract Alisoun by dressing in his best clothes and singing romantic songs under her window, completely unaware that she is in bed with Nicholas.

■ Further reading

■ The Wife of Bath's Prologue and Tale

■ The Clerk's Tale

■ The Merchant's Tale

from *The Canterbury Tales*: verse translation by Neville Coghill (Penguin) or *The Canterbury Tales*: prose translation by David Wright (Panther Books).

■ Modern language

swelte: faint

turtel: turtle dove, emblem of true love

pa: kiss

Whan that the firste cok hath crowe, anon
Up rist this joly lovere Absolon,
And hym arraieth gay, at point-devys.
But first he cheweth greyn and lycorys,
To smellen sweete, er he hadde kembd his heer.
Under his tonge a trewe-love he beer,
For therby wende he to ben gracious.
He rometh to the carpenteres hous,
And stille he stant under the shot-wyndowe –
Unto his brest it raughte, it was so lowe –
And softe he cougheth with a semysoun:
'What do ye, hony-comb, sweete Alisoun,
My faire bryd, my sweete cynamome?
Awaketh, lemman myn, and speketh to me!
Wel litel thinken ye upon my wo,
That for youre love I swete ther I go.
No wonder is thogh that I _swelte_ and swete;
I moorne as dooth a lamb aftger the tete.
Ywis, lemman, I have swich love-longynge.
That like a _turtel_ trewe is my moornynge.
I may nat ete na moore than a mayde.'
    'Go fro the wyndow, Jakke fool' she sayde;
'As help me God, it wol nat be 'com _pa_ me'.
I love another – and elles I were to blame –
Wel bet than thee, by Jhesu, Absolon.'

The Miller's Tale, lines 3687–3711

■ Questions

AO1: Developing an informed response to the text

■ What happens in the two extracts?

■ What attitudes to love are presented in them, through Nicholas and Absolon?

AO2: Understanding how structure, form and language shape meaning

■ What do you notice about the ways Chaucer uses form, structure and language in these extracts to create characters and tell the story?

AO3: Exploring connections, comparisons and the interpretations of other readers

■ Do these extracts remind you of other more modern texts that you have read, heard or seen?

AO4: Understanding of the significance and influence of contexts

Chaucer is writing in the 14th century. The context in which you are reading *The Miller's Tale* is the 21st century.

■ As a reader, would you agree that Chaucer's comedy is universal, or do you feel that too much of it depends on its period context?

■ As a reader, what makes Chaucer's comedy accessible to you, and what makes it inaccessible?

The Renaissance: the 16th century and the Elizabethans

The 16th century is a great period for love poetry, in many different forms – ode, lyric, song, and probably best known of all these, the sonnet. The Elizabethans enjoyed playing with language and ideas – they valued the exercise of **wit** in poetry (meaning intelligence and argument, not just humour) and revelled in ornate descriptions, which remind the reader of the highly decorative and stylised contemporary portraits of Queen Elizabeth. Although some of the poets in this section, or recommended as further reading, were born before Elizabeth I came to the throne, and most of them lived on after her death into the reign of James I, the label of Elizabethan is a useful one for poems mainly written during the 16th century. These authors shared similar knowledge of the traditions of love poetry, a similar education, and a preference for particular forms in which to express their ideas and feelings. The period was one of geographical and intellectual exploration and discovery, and you will see this reflected in poets' choices of language and **imagery**.

An educated young Elizabethan male would be expected to be able to produce poems about his beloved, and there were plenty of conventional models for him to use, drawing on the ideas of courtly love, with the mistress as a beautiful but unattainable goddess and the lover pining hopelessly for attention from her.

You will find examples in lyrics and songs by Thomas Lodge, Thomas Nashe and Thomas Campion. As well as conventional expressions of love, you will also find lyrics full of complaints about woman's cruelty or infidelity, like Sir Thomas Wyatt's poem which begins:

> They flee from me, that sometime did me seek
> With naked foot, stalking in my chamber.

The would-be poet could also use the **pastoral** convention, casting himself as a shepherd and his mistress as a nymph, and probably addressing her with a name traditionally used in this kind of poetry, like Phyllis, Celia, Rosalind or Phoebe.

For variations on this strand of 16th-century love poetry, look at Christopher Marlowe's *The Passionate Shepherd to His Love*, Sir Walter Raleigh's answer *The Nymph's Reply to the Shepherd*, and C. Day-Lewis's 20th-century version of Marlowe's poem, which also begins 'Come live with me and be my love'.

Fig. 4.4 The Hireling Shepherd *by William Holman Hunt (1827–1910)*

English poets discovered the sonnet through the work of the Italian poet, Petrarch (1304–74). Originally sonnets were mainly concerned with aspects of romantic love, but writers from Shakespeare onwards have used the sonnet form and structure in increasingly flexible ways, and for an increasingly wide range of subjects. In the 16th century it was fashionable to write not just single sonnets, but whole sequences of them. It was usual for these sequences to be dedicated to a patron, and not initially published for general reading, but circulated privately among the poet's friends. Apart from Shakespeare's sonnets, the best-known sequences are *Amoretti* by Edmund Spenser and *Astrophel and Stella* by Sir Philip Sidney, both of which Shakespeare would have known.

Part of the Elizabethan poets' love of language is shown in their use of extended comparisons, to illustrate their ideas. Look at this sonnet by Spenser, and think about the way he uses the comparisons of fire and ice to describe what it feels like to be in love:

> My Love is like to ice, and I to fire;
> How comes it then that this her cold so great
> Is not dissolved through my so hot desire,
> But harder grows the more I her entreat?
> Or how comes it that my exceeding heat
> Is not allayed by her heart-frozen cold,
> But that I burn much more in boiling sweat,
> And feel my flames augmented manifold?
> What more miraculous thing may be told,
> That fire, which all things melts, should harden ice,
> And ice which is congealed with senseless cold,
> Should kindle fire by wonderful device?
>   Such is the power of love in gentle mind
>   That it can alter all the course of kind.

Edmund Spenser (c.1552–1599)

The most famous sonnet sequence of the period is by William Shakespeare. Although they were probably not written in the order in which they are usually printed, his 154 sonnets appear to tell a story of love complicated by rivalry between two men, one young and attractive and the other conscious that he is ageing, for a 'dark lady' who transfers her affections from the older to the younger man, causing the poet pangs of jealousy and depression. He starts with praise and admiration of his young male patron, and then introduces themes of rejection, jealousy, depression and thoughts about death. These sonnets have been the subject of endless research and speculation about the situation they appear to describe, and the identities of the participants. It is not possible to establish any facts entirely – what we do know is that the majority of the sonnets are addressed to a man, and not to the mistress, and it is clear that as a writer Shakespeare knew the conflicting feelings of being in love, and how to present them.

Sonnet 18

Shall I compare thee to a summer's day?
Thou art more lovely and more temperate.
Rough winds do shake the darling buds of May,
And summer's lease hath all too short a date.
Sometime too hot the eye of heaven shines,
And often is his gold complexion dimmed,
And every fair from fair sometime declines,
By chance or nature's changing course untrimmed;

Further reading

- William Shakespeare (1564–1616) songs (in his comedies), sonnets (at least numbers 57, 87, 102, 116, 129, 138)
- Sir Thomas Wyatt (1503–42) *They flee from me, that sometime did me seek* and *Tangled was I in love's snare*
- Edmund Spenser (1552–91) sonnets from *Amoretti*, beginning 'Ye tradeful merchants, that, with weary toil' and 'One day I wrote her name upon the strand' and two poems celebrating marriages, *Epithalamium* and *Prothalamium*
- Sir Philip Sidney (1554–86) *My true love hath my heart, and I have his*
- Michael Drayton (1563–1631) *Since there's no help, come, let us kiss and part*
- Christopher Marlowe (1564–93) *The Passionate Shepherd to his Love*
- Sir Walter Raleigh (1552–1618) *The Nymph's Reply to the Shepherd*
- C. Day-Lewis (1904–72) *Come, live with me and be my love*
- Ovid *Metamorphoses*: prose translation by Mary Innes (Penguin), *Tales from Ovid*: 24 passages translated into poetry by Ted Hughes (Faber)

But thy eternal summer shall not fade
Nor lose possession of that fair thou ow'st,
Nor shall death brag thou wander'st in his shade
When in eternal lines to time thou grow'st.
　　So long as men can breathe or eyes can see,
　　So long lives this, and this gives life to thee.

Sonnet 90

Then hate me when thou wilt, if ever, now,
Now while the world is bent my deeds to cross,
Join with the spite of fortune, make me bow,
And do not drop in for an after-loss.
Ah do not, when my heart hath scaped this sorrow,
Come in the rearward of a conquered woe;
Give not a windy night a rainy morrow
To linger out a purposed overthrow.
If thou wilt leave me, do not leave me last,
When other petty griefs have done their spite,
But in the onset come; so shall I taste
At first the very worst of fortune's might,
　　And other strains of woe, which now seem woe,
　　Compared with lack of thee will not seem so.

Sonnet 130

My mistress' eyes are nothing like the sun;
Coral is far more red than her lips' red.
If snow be white, why then her breasts are dun;
If hairs be wires, black wires grow on her head.
I have seen roses damasked, red and white,
But no such roses see I in her cheeks,
And in some perfumes is there more delight
Than in the breath that from my mistress reeks.
I love to hear her speak, yet well I know
That music hath a far more pleasing sound.
I grant I never saw a goddess go:
My mistress when she walks treads on the ground.
　　And yet, by heaven, I think my love as rare
　　As any she belied with false compare.

William Shakespeare

Fig. 4.5 Young Man Among Roses *by Nicholas Hilliard (1547–1619)*

Questions

AO1: Developing an informed response to the text
- What thoughts and feelings are Spenser and Shakespeare expressing in each of these sonnets? Trace the train of thought in each poem.

AO2: Understanding how structure, form and language shape meaning
- With only 14 lines in which to express an idea, the poet cannot afford to waste time and words in introductions. How has the subject matter of each sonnet affected the poet's choices of language?
- How does each poet use language, form and structure to introduce, shape and develop his argument?

AO3: Exploring connections, comparisons and the interpretations of other readers
- In what ways does Spenser's sonnet differ from Shakespeare's in subject matter and style?

AO4: Understanding of the significance and influence of contexts
- How would you respond to the view of some modern critics that Elizabethan sonnets are poetic fictions, influenced more by sonnet writing conventions than by life?

The 17th century: the Metaphysical poets

The name **Metaphysical** is given to a group of poets who wrote during the first half of the 17th century and shared many approaches to love poetry with the Elizabethans, including familiarity with Classical and European literature, and awareness of the traditions of writing about love. They developed ways of weaving together forms, structure and language, combining explorations of passionate feelings with clever intellectual arguments. Above all, they shared a delight in the display of intelligence and in using language that has energy and vitality; they showed this in their continued use of elaborate and extended **similes** and images – a poetic device known as a conceit. This term means a sustained comparison and does not carry our modern meaning of arrogance and self-satisfaction, although there may be some sense of this in the tones of some of their love poetry.

The best-known and possibly most extreme example of a conceit comes at the end of *A Valediction: Forbidding Mourning* by John Donne, in which the parting lovers are compared to a pair of mathematical compasses:

> If they be so, they are two so
>   As stiff twin compasses are two,
> Thy soul, the fixed foot, makes no show
>   To move, but doth if the other do.
>
> And though it in the centre sit,
>   Yet when the other far doth roam,
> It leans and hearkens after it,
>   And grows erect, as that comes home.
>
> Such wilt thou be to me, who must
>   Like the other foot, obliquely run;
> Thy firmness draws my circle just,
>   And makes me end, where I begun.

Activity

- How do you respond to the comparison in these stanzas between the parting lovers and a pair of compasses?
- Do you find it ridiculously far-fetched, or brilliantly original?

Now read these verses in their context as the conclusion to the whole poem, printed below.

- What feelings is Donne expressing in the whole poem?
- How does the conceit contribute to the poem's effect on you?

A Valediction: Forbidding Mourning

As virtuous men pass mildly away,
    And whisper to their souls to go,
Whilst some of their sad friends do say,
    The breath goes now, and some say, no.

So let us melt, and make no noise,
    No tear-floods, nor sigh-tempests move;
'Twere profanation of our joys
    To tell the laity our love.

Moving of th' earth brings harms and fears;
    Men reckon what it did, and meant;
But trepidation of the spheres,
    Though greater far, is innocent.

Dull sublunary lovers' love
    (Whose soul is sense) cannot admit
Absence, because it doth remove
    Those things which elemented it.

But we by a love so much refined,
    That ourselves know not what it is,
Inter-assurèd of the mind,
    Care less, eyes, lips and hands to miss.

Our two souls therefore, which are one,
    Though I must go, endure not yet
A breach, but an expansion,
    Like gold to aery thinness beat.

If they be two, they are two so
    As stiff twin compasses are two;
Thy soul, the fix'd foot, makes no show
    To move, but doth, if th' other do.

And though it in the centre sit,
    Yet, when the other far doth roam,
It leans, and hearkens after it,
    And grows erect, as that comes home.

Such wilt thou be to me, who must,
    Like th' other foot, obliquely run;
Thy firmness draws my circle just,
    And makes me end where I begun.

John Donne (1572–1631)

Poems of sex and seduction: John Donne and Andrew Marvell

John Donne was born halfway through the reign of Queen Elizabeth, and died during the reign of Charles I. As a young man, Donne was known as 'a great lover of women' and the love poems written at the beginning of his career certainly seem to confirm that reputation. He was born a Catholic, but when he was nearly 50 he was ordained a priest in the Anglican Church, and ended his life as Dean of St Paul's Cathedral, leaving a legacy of great sermons and religious poems, as well as poems about love.

Meet the young John Donne – and think about the ways this poem is similar to and also different from the Elizabethan love poems you have read, especially in form and language.

Questions

AO1: Developing an informed response to the text

■ What is the setting of this poem?

AO2: Understanding how structure, form and language shape meaning

■ Trace the way Donne develops his ideas through the three verses.

■ How does Donne use his setting as part of his argument?

AO3: Exploring connections, comparisons and the interpretations of other readers

■ In what ways is this poem typical, or not typical, of the love poetry you have read so far?

AO4: Understanding of the significance and influence of contexts

■ What use does Donne make of contemporary references (for example, to geography and trade, or to current beliefs about the relationship of earth and the sun)?

The Sun Rising

Busy old fool, unruly Sun,
    Why dost thou thus,
Through windows, and through curtains, call on us?
Must to thy motions lovers' seasons run?
    Saucy pedantic wretch, go chide
    Late schoolboys and sour prentices,
  Go tell court-huntsmen that the king will ride,
  Call country ants to harvest offices;
Love, all alike, no season knows nor clime,
Nor hours, days, months which are the rags of time.

    Thy beams so reverend and strong
    Why shouldst thou think?
I could eclipse and cloud them with a wink
But that I would not lose her sight so long.
    If her eyes have not blinded thine,
    Look, and tomorrow late tell me,
  Whether both th' Indias of spice and mine
  Be where thou left'st them, or lie here with me.
Ask for those kings whom thou saw'st yesterday,
And thou shalt hear, 'All here in one bed lay.'

    She is all states, and all princes, I:
    Nothing else is;
Princes do but play us; compared to this,
All honour's mimic, all wealth alchemy.
    Thou, Sun, art half as happy as we,
    In that the world's contracted thus;
  Thine age asks ease, and since thy duties be
  To warm the world, that's done by warming us.
Shine here to us, and thou art everywhere;
This bed thy centre is, these walls thy sphere.

John Donne

Fig. 4.6 *The Ptolemaic universe. What does this image add to your understanding of the poem?*

Andrew Marvell, poet and politician, lived through the Civil War and saw the restoration of Charles II to the throne in 1660.

Modern language

chaps: jaws

slow-chapt: slowly devouring

To His Coy Mistress

Had we but world enough, and time,
This coyness, Lady, were no crime.
We would sit down, and think which way
To walk, and pass our long love's day.
Thou by the Indian Ganges' side
Should'st rubies find: I by the tide
Of Humber would complain. I would
Love you ten years before the Flood,
And you should, if you please, refuse
Till the conversion of the Jews.
My vegetable love should grow
Vaster than empires, and more slow;
An hundred years should go to praise
Thine eyes and on thy forehead gaze;
Two hundred to adore each breast;
But thirty thousand to the rest;
An age at least to every part,
And the last age should show your heart;
For, Lady, you deserve this state,
Nor would I love at lower rate.
    But at my back I always hear
Time's wingèd chariot hurrying near:
And yonder all before us lie
Deserts of vast eternity.
Thy beauty shall no more be found,
Nor, in thy marble vault, shall sound
My echoing song: then worms shall try
That long preserved virginity,
And your quaint honour turn to dust,
And into ashes all my lust:
The grave's a fine and private place,
But none, I think, do there embrace.
    Now therefore, while the youthful hue
Sits on thy skin like morning dew,
And while thy willing soul transpires
At every pore with instant fires,
Now let us sport us while we may;
And now, like amorous birds of prey,
Rather at once our time devour
Than languish in his slow-chapt power.
 Let us roll all our strength and all
Our sweetness up into one ball,
And tear our pleasures with rough strife
Thorough the iron gates of life:
Thus, though we cannot make our sun
Stand still, yet we will make him run.

Andrew Marvell (1621–78)

Questions

AO1: Developing an informed response to the text
- What is the situation in *To His Coy Mistress*?

AO2: Understanding how structure, form and language shape meaning
- 'Time' is a key word in this poem. Explore the ways Marvell refers to and describes time, and his use of these ideas as part of his argument.
- Look at Marvell's choices of words and phrases which highlight the woman's virginity, 'coyness' and her sexual attractiveness, and the speaker's 'lust'.
  - Do any words or phrases strike you as odd in this poem?
  - Why, for example, does he call his love his 'vegetable' love?
  - What is the point of his references to the Flood, and the 'conversion of the Jews'?

- How do you interpret the images in the final lines of the poem?
- Trace the stages of Marvell's argument. What use does he make of variations in tone and pace as part of his persuasive technique?

AO3: Exploring connections, comparisons and the interpretations of other readers
- What links can you make between this poem and any others that you have studied, in terms of attitudes to love, themes and styles?

AO4: Understanding of the significance and influence of contexts
- In what ways do you think this poem is typical of its time?

Poems like *To His Coy Mistress*, which emphasise the shortness of life and the transience of beauty, are often called **'seize the day'** poems. You will find more examples in the poems of the Cavalier poets, young men who were associated with the court of Charles I and supported the King during the Civil War, such as Robert Herrick, Edmund Waller, John Suckling and Richard Lovelace.

Poems of love, marriage and death: Anne Bradstreet and Bishop Henry King

Anne Bradstreet was a Puritan, who was born in England but emigrated to America with her family in 1630, where her husband became Governor of the colony of Massachusetts. During her lifetime her poems were published anonymously.

To my dear and loving husband

If ever two were one, then surely we.
If ever man were loved by wife, then thee;
If ever wife was happy in a man,
Compare with me, ye women, if you can.
I prize thy love more than whole mines of gold,
Or all the riches that the East doth hold.
My love is such that rivers cannot quench,
Nor aught but love from thee give recompense.
Thy love is such I can no way repay;
The heavens reward thee manifold, I pray.
Then while we live, in love let's so persever,
That when we live no more, we may live ever.

Anne Bradstreet (1612–72)

Like Marvell, Bishop Henry King lived through the Civil War. During it he was deprived of his bishopric by the Puritans, but reinstated during the reign of Charles II. He wrote a number of poems addressed to his wife after her death. Here are two extracts from his long poem *The Exequy*, which is sometimes subtitled, 'To his matchless never to be forgotten friend'. The first extract is the opening of the poem; the second is from the final section.

Extract 1 from *The Exequy*

Accept, thou shrine of my dead saint
Instead of dirges this complaint;
And for sweet flowers to crown thy hearse
Receive a strew of weeping verse
From thy grieved friend, whom thou might'st see
Quite melted into tears for thee.

Extract 2 from *The Exequy*

Sleep on, my Love, in thy cold bed
Never to be disquieted.
My last good night! Thou wilt not wake
Till I thy fate shall overtake:
Till age, or grief, or sickness must
Marry my body to that dust
It so much loves; and fill the room
My heart keeps empty in thy tomb.

Further reading

John Donne *The Good Morrow, The Flea, To His Mistress Going to Bed, A Valediction Forbidding Mourning, Nocturnal on St Lucy's Day, The Relique, The Anniversarie, Twickenham Garden*

Robert Herrick (1591–1674) *To virgins to make much of time*

Edmund Waller (1606–87) *Go, lovely rose, On a Girdle*

Sir John Suckling (1609–42) *Why so pale and wan, fair lover?, The Constant Lover*

Richard Lovelace (1618–68) *To Lucasta, On Going to the Wars*

Married love poems

Henry King (1592–1669) *The Surrender*

John Milton (1608–74) *Methought I saw my late espoused saint*

Matthew Arnold (1822–88) *On Dover Beach*

Philip Larkin (1922–85) *An Arundel Tomb*

Elizabeth Jennings (1926–2001) *One flesh*

Definitions of love

Sir Walter Raleigh *As you came from the Holy Land*

William Shakespeare, Sonnets 116, 130

Andrew Marvell (1621–78) *A Definition of Love*

e e cummings (1894–1962) *Love is more thicker than forget*

Adrian Henri (1932–2000) *Love is …*

Stay for me there: I will not fail
To meet thee in that hollow vale.
And think not much of my delay;
I am already on the way,
And follow thee with all the speed
Desire can make, or sorrows breed.
Each minute is a short degree,
And ev'ry hour a step towards thee.
At night when I betake to rest,
Next morn I rise nearer my west
Of life, almost by eight hours' sail,
Than when sleep breath'd his drowsy gale.
    Thus from the sun my <u>bottom</u> steers,
And my day's compass downward bears:
Nor labour I to stem the tide
Through which to thee I swiftly glide.
    'Tis true, with shame and grief I yield,
Thou like the <u>van</u> first took'st the field,
And gotten hast the victory
In thus adventuring to die
Before me, whose more years might crave
A just precedence in the grave.
But hark! my pulse, like a soft drum
Beats my approach, tells thee I come;
And slow howe're my marches be,
I shall at last sit down by thee.

Henry King (1592–1669)

Modern language

bottom: boat

van: vanguard, leader

Questions

AO1: Developing an informed response to the text
- What thoughts and feelings are Bradstreet and King expressing in these poems?

AO2: Understanding how structure, form and language shape meaning
- Trace the ways Henry King develops his train of thought through the extracts.

AO3: Exploring connections, comparisons and the interpretations of other readers
- Compare the different effects which Donne, Marvell and King create through their uses of form and 'voice' in their poems.
- In the 18th century the Metaphysical poets were criticised for 'showing off' in their poetry, by forcing comparisons between things that have almost nothing in common. On the basis of these poems, do you agree with that, or how would you defend them?

AO4: Understanding of the significance and influence of contexts
- What use does King make of contemporary references?

The 18th century and the Romantics

Pope, Keats and Byron

Poets in the 18th century largely turned against the styles and popular subjects of earlier periods. In general they were more concerned with religion and politics, but love never disappears entirely. The light-hearted, satirical **mock heroic epic**, *The Rape of the Lock*, by Alexander Pope, is based on a real-life incident when a young nobleman stole a lock of hair from a society beauty, causing a feud between their families. This poem deals with sexual attraction, an act of what today we would call sexual harassment, and, literally, the battle of the sexes.

Towards the end of the century 'love' again becomes a major poetic theme, and among the Romantic poets, Keats and Byron are arguably the most 'romantic' in the 20th-century sense of the word. The stories that Keats tells in his narrative poems are love stories, the facts about his life and early death, and his love for Fanny Brawne, are romantic ones, and in his poetry he is explicit about feelings and emotions. Consider his sensuous fantasy of an elopement in *The Eve of St Agnes*; the different kinds of tragedy in *Isabella* and *Lamia*; and his doomed love for Fanny, in his last sonnet:

Bright star! would I were steadfast as thou art

Bright star! would I were steadfast as thou art –
  Not in lone splendour hung aloft the night
And watching, with eternal lids apart,
  Like Nature's patient, sleepless <u>Eremite</u>,
The moving waters at their priestlike task
  Of pure ablution round earth's human shores,
Or gazing on the new soft fallen mask
  Of snow upon the mountains and the moors –
No – yet still steadfast, still unchangeable,
  Pillowed upon my fair love's ripening breast,
To feel forever its soft fall and swell,
  Awake forever in a sweet unrest,
Still, still to hear her tender-taken breath,
And so live ever – or else swoon to death.

John Keats (1795–1821)

Modern language

Eremite: hermit

Love and romance are naturally recurrent topics in Byron's long narrative poem *Don Juan*. Don Juan is the hero of many plays, poems, operas and stories in European literature, in all of which he is a heartless and immoral seducer of women. Byron subverts this character by making his hero an innocent teenager at the beginning of the poem; in the stories of Juan's many love affairs during his travels, the young man is more often the victim of women than their downfall.

Byron chooses an Italian verse form, the **ottava rima**, to create an extraordinarily flexible narrative voice for his combination of storytelling and personal commentaries on the action.

In the following stanzas from Canto 1, Juan is being seduced by his mother's friend, Julia.

(…) shows that some stanzas have been omitted.

How beautiful she looked! Her conscious heart
Glowed in her cheek, and yet she felt no wrong.
Oh Love, how perfect is thy mystic art,
  Strengthening the weak and trampling on the strong.
How self-deceitful is the sagest part
  Of mortals whom thy lure hath led along.

The precipice she stood on was immense,
So was her creed in her own innocence.

She thought of her own strength and Juan's youth
   And of the folly of all prudish fears,
Victorious virtue and domestic truth,
   And then of Don Alfonso's fifty years.
I wish these last had not occurred in sooth,
   Because that number rarely much endears
And through all climes, the snowy and the sunny,
Sounds ill in love, whate'er it may in money.
(…)
Julia had honour, virtue, truth and love
   For Don Alfonso, and she inly swore
By all the vows below to powers above,
   She never would disgrace the ring she wore
Nor leave a wish which wisdom might reprove.
   And while she pondered this, besides much more,
One hand on Juan's carelessly was thrown,
Quite by mistake – she thought it was her own.

Unconsciously she leaned upon the other,
   Which played within the tangles of her hair.
And to contend with thoughts she could not smother,
   She seemed by the distraction of her air.
'Twas surely very wrong in Juan's mother
   To leave together this imprudent pair,
She who for many years had watched her son so.
I'm very certain mine would not have done so.
(…)
I cannot know what Juan thought of this,
   But what he did was much what you would do.
His young lip thanked it with a grateful kiss
   And then abashed at its own joy withdrew
In deep despair, lest he had done amiss.
   Love is so very timid when 'tis new.
She blushed and frowned not, but she strove to speak
And held her tongue, her voice was grown so weak.
(…)
And Julia sate with Juan, half embraced
   And half retiring from the glowing arm,
Which trembled like the bosom where 'twas placed.
   Yet still she must have thought there was no harm,
Or else 'twere easy to withdraw her waist.
   But then the situation had its charm,
And then – God knows what next – I can't go on;
I'm almost sorry that I e'er begun.
 (…)
And Julia's voice was lost, except in sighs,
   Until too late for useful conversation.
The tears were gushing from her gentle eyes;
   I wish indeed they had not had occasion,
But who, alas, can love and then be wise?
   Not that remorse did not oppose temptation;
A little still she strove and much repented,
And whispering, 'I will ne'er consent' – consented.

George Gordon, Lord Byron (1788–1824)

Further reading

- Alexander Pope (1688–1744) *The Rape of the Lock*
- William Wordsworth (1770–1850) *The Lucy poems*: 'Strange fits of passion I have known', 'She dwelt among the untrodden ways', 'I travell'd among unknown men', 'Three years she grew in sun and shower', 'A slumber did my spirit seal', 'She was a phantom of delight', 'It is a beauteous evening, calm and free'
- Samuel Taylor Coleridge (1772–1834) *Frost at Midnight* (parent and child)
- John Keats (1795–1821) *La Belle Dame sans Merci, The Eve of St Agnes, Isabella, Lamia*
- Percy Bysshe Shelley (1792–1822) love lyrics, *One word is too often profaned, Music when soft voices die, I arise from dreams of thee, The fountains mingle with the river*
- George Gordon, Lord Byron (1788–1824) shorter lyrics, *She walks in beauty, like the night, So we'll go no more a roving, When we two parted*

Questions

AO1: Developing an informed response to the text

- In Keats' sonnet, and the extract from *Don Juan*, what are the poets' thoughts and feelings about love?

AO2: Understanding how structure, form and language shape meaning

- Explore the poets' uses of form, structure and language.
- What are the differences in tone, and how are these achieved?
- What do you notice particularly about the ways in which Byron uses language in these stanzas?

AO3: Exploring connections, comparisons and the interpretations of other readers

- Does the extract from *Don Juan* remind you of any other texts you have read?
- How far do you agree with the view that prose would be a more appropriate genre for this episode than poetry?
- Compare the tone and content of the extract from *Don Juan* with any of Byron's shorter lyrics about love.

AO4: Understanding of the significance and influence of contexts

- Which context – literary, social, historical or biographical – seems most relevant to you in reading and understanding these poems by Keats and Byron?

The Victorians

Today we tend to use the term 'Victorian values' to mean reactionary and extremely conservative views about morality and the roles of women, and to laugh at what seems to be a prudish reluctance to be explicit about feelings of love and passion. After Byron, much Victorian poetry about love may seem sentimental, but close reading will reveal strong undercurrents of passionate feelings. If you studied the Victorians as your AS option you will already have had a good introduction to the love poetry of the period. If you did not study that option, you will find the chapter on Victorian poetry in the Nelson Thornes *AQA English Literature A: Victorian Literature AS* book helpful. The sections on Elizabeth Barrett Browning and Emily Dickinson will be particularly useful to you.

Women's poetry: Christina Rossetti and Emily Dickinson – English and American contemporaries

Elizabeth Barrett Browning's *Sonnets from the Portuguese* are a sustained exploration of her love for Robert Browning. Her main focus is on the immediacy of her feelings for him, and this is reflected in her language. Other Victorian women poets seem more concerned with the transience of life, the inevitability of death and themes of nostalgia, renunciation, or the continuation of love after death, and poems by women celebrating love in the way Barrett Browning does are fairly rare during this period.

A Birthday

My heart is like a singing bird
   Whose nest is in a watered shoot;
My heart is like an apple tree
   Whose bough is bent with thick set fruit;
My heart is like a rainbow shell
   That paddles in a halcyon sea;
My heart is gladder than all these
   Because my love is come to me.

Raise me a dais of silk and down;
   Hang it with vair and purple dyes;
Carve it with doves and pomegranates,
   And peacocks with a hundred eyes;

Work it in gold and silver grapes,
    In leaves and silver fleur-de-lys;
Because the birthday of my life
    Is come, my love is come to me.

Christina Rossetti (1831–94)

Remember

Remember me when I am gone away,
Gone far away into the silent land;
When you can no more hold me by the hand,
Nor I half turn to go, yet turning stay.
Remember me when no more, day by day,
You tell me of our future that you planned;
Only remember me; you understand
It will be late to counsel then or pray.
Yet if you should forget me for a while
And afterwards remember, do not grieve;
For if the darkness and corruption leave
A vestige of the thoughts that once I had,
Better by far you should forget and smile
Than that you should remember and be sad.

Christina Rossetti

Love's stricken 'why'

Love's stricken 'why'
Is all that love can speak –
Built of but just a syllable
The hugest hearts that break.

Emily Dickinson (1830–86)

My life closed twice

My life closed twice before its close;
It yet remains to see
If Immortality unveil
A third event to me,

So huge, so hopeless to conceive
As these that twice befell.
Parting is all we know of heaven,
And all we need of hell.

Emily Dickinson

Fig. 4.7 Romeo and Juliet *by Ford Maddox Brown (1821–1893)*

Poems by men: Alfred, Lord Tennyson; Robert Browning; Thomas Hardy; W.B. Yeats

Tennyson and Browning are both solidly Victorian, and much better known for long narrative poems and dramatic monologues than for short lyrics. *Now sleeps the crimson petal* is a lyric which Tennyson embedded in a longer romantic narrative poem, *The Princess; Meeting at Night* is an uncharacteristically short and directly expressed poem by Browning, written during 1845, the year he first met Elizabeth Barrett.

Although Hardy and Yeats were both born halfway through the 19th century, they both lived through World War One and well into the 20th century. Consequently, as poets, the label of 'Victorian' does not fit either of them very comfortably. Yeats wrote *When you are old and grey* at the end of the 19th century, and Hardy wrote *The Voice* at the beginning of the 20th century, after the death of his wife.

Now sleeps the crimson petal, now the white

Now sleeps the crimson petal, now the white
Nor waves the cypress in the palace walk;
Nor winks the gold fin in the porphyry font:
The firefly wakens: waken thou with me.

Now droops the milk-white peacock like a ghost,
And like a ghost she glimmers on to me.

Now lies the earth all Danae to the stars,
And all thy heart lies open unto me.

Now slides the silent meteor on, and leaves
A shining furrow, as thy thoughts in me.

Now folds the lily all her sweetness up,
And slips into the bosom of the lake:
So fold thyself, my dearest, thou, and slip
Into my bosom and be lost in me.

Alfred, Lord Tennyson (1809–92)

Meeting at Night

The grey sea and the long black land;
And the yellow half-moon large and low;
And the startled little waves that leap
In fiery ringlets from their sleep,
As I gain the cove with pushing prow,
And quench its speed in the slushy sand.

Then a mile of warm sea-scented beach;
Three fields to cross till a farm appears;
A tap at the pane, the quick sharp scratch
And blue spurt of a lighted match,
And a voice less loud, through its joys and fears,
Than two hearts beating each to each.

Robert Browning (1812–89)

The Voice

Woman much missed, how you call to me, call to me,
Saying that now you are not as you were
When you had changed from the one who was all to me,
But as at first, when our day was fair.

Can it be you that I hear? Let me view you, then,
Standing as when I drew near to the town
Where you would wait for me: yes, as I knew you then,
Even to the original air-blue gown!

Further reading

Elizabeth Barrett Browning (1806–61) *Sonnets from the Portuguese*, especially numbers XIV (14), XXI (21), XXXII (32), XXXVIII (38), XLIII (43)

Christina Rossetti: (1830–94) *Goblin Market* (love between sisters)

Emily Dickinson (1830–86)

Alice Meynell (1847–1922) *Renouncement*

Alfred, Lord Tennnyson (1809–92) *Mariana* (unrequited love), *Maud* (obsessive love), *In Memoriam* sections VI (6), VII (7), XVIII (18), CXXIX (109), CXXX (130) (Queen Victoria's favourite poem, about love and male friendship)

Robert Browning (1812–89) *Porphyria's Lover, My Last Duchess, The Laboratory, Andrea del Sarto, In a Gondola, Two in the Campagna, The Last Ride Together* (a 'live for the moment' poem)

Coventry Patmore (1823–96) *The Toys* (father and child)

Thomas Hardy (1840–1928) prose and poetry. Poems 1912–13 *The Going, The Walk, The Haunter, After a Journey* (to his wife), *Time of the Breaking of Nations*

W.B. Yeats (1865–1939) *He wishes for the cloths of heaven, Prayer for my Daughter*

Or is it only the breeze, in its listlessness
Travelling across the wet mead to me here,
You being ever dissolved to wan wistlessness,
Heard no more again far or near?

   Thus I; faltering forward,
   Leaves around me falling,
Wind oozing thin through the thorn from norward,
   And the woman calling.

Thomas Hardy (1840–1928)

When you are old and grey and full of sleep

When you are old and grey and full of sleep,
And nodding by the fire, take down this book,
And slowly read, and dream of the soft look
Your eyes had once, and of their shadows deep;

How many loved your moments of glad grace,
And loved your beauty with love false or true,
But one man loved the pilgrim soul in you,
And loved the sorrows of your changing face;

And bending down beside the glowing bars,
Murmur, a little sadly, how Love fled
And paced upon the mountains overhead
And hid his face amid a crowd of stars.

W.B. Yeats (1865–1939)

Questions

AO1: Developing an informed response to the text
- What different aspects of love are these poems by men and women about?

AO2: Understanding how structure, form and language shape meaning
- What similarities and differences do you find in the moods of the poets, and the styles in which they express them?

AO3: Exploring connections, comparisons and the interpretations of other readers
- What links can you see with other poems about love which you have read, either from the Victorian period or from other periods?
- How far would you agree with the view that Victorian poets are sentimentally preoccupied with death in their love poetry, and that real feelings and passion are outside their range?

- It has been said that Thomas Hardy is a Victorian novelist, but a modern poet. As far as his poetry is concerned, would you agree with this view, and for what reasons? If you have also read some of Hardy's novels, how far would you agree, in relation to his prose?

AO4: Understanding of the significance and influence of contexts
- How important do you think the gender of the writer is in these poems?
- How significant and useful do you find dates of composition when setting poems in context?
- Which of these poems would you describe as typically Victorian, and why? Which strike you as 'modern', and why?

◱ The 20th and 21st centuries: contemporary love poetry

If you studied the Victorian option for AS, you will be very aware of differences between 19th-century and modern poetry about love. If you studied the World War One option you will know how much the experience of the Great War changed literature and society. If you studied the Struggle for Identity in Modern Literature option, you will understand more about how and why the context of social and political change affects the literature of the 20th and 21st centuries. In his poem *Annus Mirabilis* Philip Larkin dates change very precisely; according to him, it happened in 1963 when, he says, 'sexual intercourse began'. Since then contemporary poets have certainly written about all aspects of love much more explicitly and in a great variety of forms and styles, but poets did not have to wait until 1963 to do this.

Here is a lyric poem by the American poet, e e cummings, drawing on his experience in World War One, in which he was an ambulance driver. Please note that nothing has gone wrong with the layout and printing of this poem! cummings often used traditional forms, like the sonnet and the lyric, but because he wanted the layout of his poems to be an essential part of their moods and meanings, he abandoned capitalisation and conventional punctuation in his experiments with the visual appearance of his poems on the page.

my sweet old etcetera

my sweet old etcetera
aunt lucy during the recent

war could and what
is more did tell you just
what everybody was fighting

for,
my sister

isabel created hundreds
(and
hundreds) of socks not to
mention shirts fleaproof earwarmers

etcetera wristers etcetera, my
mother hoped that

I would die etcetera
bravely of course my father used
to become hoarse talking about how it was
a privilege and if only he
could meanwhile my

self etcetera lay quietly
in the deep mud et

cetera
(dreaming,
et
   cetera, of
Your smile
eyes knees and of your Etcetera)

e e cummings (1894–1962)

Questions

AO1: Developing an informed response to the text
- What is cummings' poem about?

AO2: Understanding how structure, form and language shape meaning
- What is your reaction to the ways that cummings uses form, structure and language?

AO3: Exploring connections, comparisons and the interpretations of other readers
- Can you find any links and connections between this poem and other poems about love which you have read?

AO4: Understanding of the significance and influence of contexts
- How does cummings use the context of World War One?

◼ Further reading

It is hard to think of any of the poets who are best known today who do not write some poems about love. Here is a list of modern poets, with some suggestions of starting points for your own exploration of contemporary poetry of love.

e e cummings (1894–1962) *Selected Poems* (Penguin): *i like my body when it is with your body* (a sonnet), *may I feel said he* (a dialogue? a narrative? a love poem?)

From *Scars Upon My Heart: Women's poetry and verse of the First World War*, ed. Catherine Reilly (Virago) love poems by Marian Allen, Vera Brittain, May Wedderburn Cannan, Margaret Postgate Cole, Teresa Hooley, Katharine Tynan, Marjorie Wilson

Ogden Nash (American comic poet, 1902–71) *To my Valentine*

W.H. Auden (1907–73) *Lay your sleeping head, my love*

Robert Hayden (African-American poet 1913–80) from *101 Sonnets*, ed. Don Paterson (Faber): *Those Winter Sundays* (father and son)

Philip Larkin (1922–85) from *Collected Poems* (Faber): *An Arundel Tomb, Love Songs in Age*

Elizabeth Jennings (1926–2001) (parents and old age) *One Flesh*

Adrienne Rich (American poet 1929–) from *Twenty One Love Poems*: No II *I wake up in your bed. I know I have been dreaming*

Adrian Henri (1932–2000) from *The Mersey Sound* (Penguin): *Without you, Where'er you walk, In the midnight hour, Love is …*

Sylvia Plath (1932–63) from *Collected Poems* (Faber): *You're, Nick and the Candlestick, Balloons* (mother and children)

Ted Hughes (1930–98) *Birthday Letters* (Faber)

Fleur Adcock (1934–) *The Chiffonier* (daughter and mother)

Tony Harrison (1937–) from *Selected Poems* (Penguin): *Book Ends I & II, Long Distance I & II, Illuminations I & II, Isolation* (sonnets to his parents)

Douglas Dunn (1942–) *Elegies* (Faber) (to his wife)

Wendy Cope (1945–) poems from *Making Cocoa for Kingsley Amis* and *Serious Concerns* (Faber)

Simon Armitage (1963–) from *Selected Poems* (Faber): *Mother, any distance greater than a single span* (son and mother)

Carol Anne Duffy (1955–) poems from *Meantime* (Anvil) and *The World's Wife* (Picador): Valentine, Anne Hathaway, Havisham; *Rapture* (Picador)

Jackie Kay (1961–) poems from *Darling* (Bloodaxe)

🔍💡 Conclusion

To conclude this survey of love poetry across the ages, here are two poems which have double vision. Think about the ways in which they link back to the literature of the distant and more recent past in subject matter and styles, while their contexts are completely contemporary.

Thom Gunn was English, but lived for most of his life in San Francisco. *Terminal* comes from his collection of poems, *The Man With Night Sweats*, published in 1992, which contains many poems dedicated to friends who had died of Aids.

Terminal

The eight years difference in age seems now
Disparity so wide between the two
That when I see the man who armoured stood
Resistant to all help however good
Now helped through day itself, eased into chairs,
Or else led step by step down the long stairs
With firm and gentle guidance by his friend,
Who loves him, through each effort to descend,
Each wavering, each attempt made to complete
An arc of movement and bring down the feet
As if with that spare strength he used to enjoy,
I think of Oedipus, old, led by a boy.

Thom Gunn (1929 –2004)

Wendy Cope's love poetry is usually witty and fairly light-hearted. *Spared* was written following the attack on the Twin Towers in 2001.

Spared

*'That love is all there is,
Is all we know of Love…'* – Emily Dickinson

It wasn't you, it wasn't me,
Up there, two thousand feet above
The New York street. We're safe, and free,
A little while, to live and love,

Imagining what might have been –
The phone call from the blazing tower,
A last farewell on the machine,
While someone sleeps another hour,

Or worse, perhaps, to say goodbye
And listen to each other's pain,
Send helpless love across the sky,
Knowing we'll never meet again,

Or jump together, hand in hand,
To certain death. Spared all of this,
For now, how well I understand
That love is all, is all there is.

Wendy Cope (1945–)

Summary

In working through this chapter you have begun to develop an overview of love poetry from Chaucer to the present day, by focusing on:

- major poets, literary traditions and individual writers' styles

- ways of linking poems within and across different periods

- your skills of close reading, analysis and interpretation of texts.

5 Prose about love

Introduction

In this chapter we are going to explore prose extracts through time which have **love** as their theme. At AS, you studied one prose text in detail in your coursework unit, and, no doubt, read many more prose texts in your preparation for the context question. This reading in prose was within your chosen **shared context** – either Victorian Literature, or World War One Literature, or Modern Literature on the theme of The Struggle for Identity. You will no doubt have come across writing about love in your AS reading, and that would perhaps be a good place to start in your reflection on and consideration of the ways writers treat the theme in their prose writing.

The centrality of the novel in this chapter and an attempt at definition

In this chapter, we intend to signpost the possible excursions you might want to take down the sub-genre side-roads of diaries, letters, memoirs, **polemic** or short stories; but the main road of this chapter is going to pass through significant moments in the history of the **novel** from the 18th century to the present day.

Perhaps the first thing we should do is to find a working **definition** of the novel. Of course this sounds quite straightforward, but it is not. Probably we can agree that all novels are dependent on catching and then sustaining the reader's interest and willingness to read on; and that reading a novel is a complex and engaging experience which invites us to become interested in and sympathetic to a variety of characters. However, that might be the limit of what we can agree on, especially as the novel as a genre has developed through time. For instance, in his book, *The English Novel An Introduction*, Terry Eagleton attempts a definition – 'The novel is a piece of prose fiction of a reasonable length' – and then proceeds to argue it down. He points out that not all novels are written in prose; that the distinction between fact and fiction is not always clear; and that it is difficult to define 'reasonable length'. He puts forward the idea that it is very tricky to define a novel because it is a sort of 'anti-genre' that steals from and mixes together other genres.

In the light of this difficulty, perhaps it would be sensible to review our 'definitions' as we travel through time in this chapter. We will start with the statement that the traditional narrative has a speaker/writer who communicates to the reader in continuous prose a series of events in chronological order. This is very much in line with E. M. Forster's view that a novel is a succession of events arranged in their time sequence and ending with what William Golding referred to as a satisfactory conclusion. We will monitor the usefulness of this definition as we move through the chapter and consider important developments in the novel.

Your reading log

Not only will you need to keep reviewing the definition of the novel, but throughout your work in this chapter you will need to keep a log.

Link

To remind yourself of the list of questions for analysing a text, turn back to pp5–6.

Link

For more information on the wider reading portfolio, see Chapter 1.

Further reading

An Anthology of Elizabethan Prose Fiction, ed. Paul Salzman (Oxford World Classics)

Oroonoko, The Rover and Other Works by Aphra Behn (Penguin Classics)

Love Letters, An Anthology chosen by Antonia Fraser (Weidenfeld and Nicolson)

Whether you use the online resources, or a paper file, such record keeping is vital as it will become your revision tool for the examination. What we can offer you in one chapter is but a small taste of the great prose riches of English literature, but what we are trying to demonstrate is development through time and tradition. You need to have a method that will enable you to keep a **log** of your reading which records both **genre and time**. The grid in the Appendix is there to help you.

As you study the extracts that follow, questions are provided to help you, but for a fuller analytical study of an extract or whole text remember to use the questions in Chapter 1.

Don't forget to also keep your **wider reading portfolio** up to date.

Prose about love through the ages

Before the 18th century

It is unlikely that you will want to follow the narrow footpaths into 16th- and 17th-century prose works in your reading for Unit 3, but if your interests take you this way, there are **diaries** (Pepys', for example) and **letters** (Henry VIII's to Anne Boleyn, for example). There is also the work of the poet, playwright and novelist Aphra Behn who died in 1689. Virginia Woolf wrote of Behn in *A Room of One's Own*: 'All women together ought to let flowers fall upon the tomb of Aphra Behn, for it was she who earned them the right to speak their minds'. Behn is generally regarded as the pioneer of the genre of the novel. If you explore her writings you will find that **love** is a central concern of her work. For example, her novel, *The Fair Jilt*, begins with these words: 'As love is the most noble and divine passion of the soul, so is it that to which we may justly attribute all the real satisfactions of life, and without it, man is unfinished, and unhappy'.

18th-century beginnings

At the beginning of the 18th century there was a wide range of books and stories, variously known as 'romances', 'histories' or 'true histories'. The first novels were so called in the 18th century because they were 'novel' in the sense of being a 'new' genre. Their chief aim seemed to be to achieve '**realism**'; the writing was characterised by detailed descriptions of settings and by a clear causal link between character and plot.

Defoe is usually credited with writing the first novels – the first-person prose fictions *Moll Flanders* and *Robinson Crusoe*. But it is true to say that Richardson (1689–1761) and Fielding (1707–54) saw themselves as founders of the novel. Their approaches to writing narratives are, however, very different.

Let's start with Fielding, and with his novel *Tom Jones* published in 1749. Fielding's approach is generally regarded as that of a 'moral comedian'. In Book Two of *Tom Jones* he described himself as the 'founder of a new province of writing'. He reaches for a classical model, claiming to be writing a comic epic in prose, but he departs from this model by introducing people from the lower classes. The novel traces the **picaresque** adventures of the eponymous hero on the road to London and his adventures there. In the following extract he meets a certain Mrs Waters at an inn; he is, however, in love with Sophia.

Extract A from *Tom Jones*

All the graces which young ladies and young gentlemen too learn from others, and the many improvements which, by the help of a looking-glass, they add of their own, are in reality those very specula et faces amoris so often mentioned by Ovid; or, as they are sometimes called in our own language, the whole artillery of love.

Now Mrs. Waters and our heroe had no sooner sat down together than the former began to play this artillery upon the latter. But here, as we are about to attempt a description hitherto unassayed either in prose or verse, we think proper to invoke the assistance of certain aerial beings, who will, we doubt not, come kindly to our aid on this occasion.

Say then, ye Graces! You that inhabit the heavenly mansions of Seraphina's countenance; for you are truly divine, are always in her presence, and well know all the arts of charming; say, what were the weapons now used to captivate the heart of Mr. Jones.

First, from two lovely blue eyes, whose bright orbs flashed lightning at their discharge, flew forth two pointed ogles; but, happily for our heroe, hit only a vast piece of beef which he was then conveying into his plate, and harmless spent their force. The fair warrior perceived their miscarriage, and immediately from her fair bosom drew forth a deadly sigh. A sigh which none could have heard unmoved, and which was sufficient at once to have swept off a dozen beaus; so soft, so sweet, so tender, that the insinuating air must have found its subtle way to the heart of our heroe, had it not luckily been driven from his ears by the coarse bubbling of some bottled ale, which at that time he was pouring forth. Many other weapons did she assay; but the god of eating (if there be any such deity, for I do not confidently assert it) preserved his votary; or perhaps it may not be dignus vindice nodus, and the present security of Jones may be accounted for by natural means; for as love frequently preserves from the attacks of hunger, so may hunger possibly, in some cases, defend us against love.

The fair one, enraged at her frequent disappointments, determined on a short cessation of arms. Which interval she employed in making ready every engine of amorous warfare for the renewing of the attack when dinner should be over.

No sooner then was the cloth removed than she again began her operations. First, having planted her right eye sidewise against Mr. Jones, she shot from its corner a most penetrating glance; which, though great part of its force was spent before it reached our heroe, did not vent itself absolutely without effect. This the fair one perceiving, hastily withdrew her eyes, and levelled them downwards, as if she was concerned for what she had done; though by this means she designed only to draw him from his guard, and indeed to open his eyes, through which she intended to surprise his heart. And now, gently lifting up those two bright orbs which had already begun to make an impression on poor Jones, she discharged a volley of small charms at once from her whole countenance in a smile. Not a smile of mirth, nor of joy; but a smile of affection, which most ladies have always ready at their command, and which serves them to show at once their good-humour, their pretty dimples, and their white teeth.

This smile our heroe received full in his eyes, and was immediately staggered with its force. He then began to see the designs of the enemy, and indeed to feel their success. A parley now was set on foot between the parties; during which the artful fair so slily and imperceptibly carried on her attack, that she had almost subdued the heart of our heroe before she again repaired to acts of hostility. To confess the truth, I am afraid Mr. Jones maintained a kind of Dutch defence, and treacherously delivered up the garrison, without duly weighing his allegiance to the fair Sophia. In short, no sooner had the amorous parley ended and the lady had unmasked the royal battery, by carelessly letting her handkerchief drop from her neck, than the heart of Mr. Jones was entirely taken, and the fair conqueror enjoyed the usual fruits of her victory.

Tom Jones, Book ix Chapter v

Fig. 5.1 *Tom with an amorous-looking Mrs Waters*

Questions

AO1: Developing an informed response to the text

■ Describe what is happening between the two people.

■ What do you learn about the two people and their relationship?

AO2: Understanding how form, structure and language shape meaning

■ What effect does Fielding's description of these events have on you, the reader?

■ Starting with the word *artillery*, trace the use of military **metaphor** through the passage and analyse its effects.

■ Comment on what the writer does **not** describe.

AO3: Exploring connections, comparisons and the interpretations of other readers

■ Compare this passage with other descriptions of lovers enjoying a meal together – look, for example, at the final dinner party in *Larry's Party* by Carol Shields, or at the picnic so carefully prepared at the beginning of *Enduring Love* by Ian McEwan.

■ Terry Eagleton considers that 'what fashions Tom Jones' destiny is not so much Tom himself, as the plot in which he finds himself caught up'. On the basis of your reading of this passage, how far do you agree?

■ How far do you agree that Fielding's style has much in common with that of Chaucer?

AO4: Understanding the significance and influence of contexts

■ How is the writer influenced by the 18th-century context?

■ What are the attitudes to love displayed in the extract?

We will now move on to look at Richardson, and to compare the work of the two writers. In order to explore their different approaches to the construction of character and representation of society we are going to look at two extracts, one from *Pamela* (Book One published 1740, Book Two 1741) by Richardson and *Shamela* (published 1741) by Fielding.

Pamela is an **epistolary** novel tracing the story, development and growth of a servant girl whose mistress dies. Mr B becomes head of the household and pursues Pamela who writes long letters to her parents describing her experiences as they happen. Pamela resists his advances, and eventually they marry. Book Two describes her way of adapting to her new life. This book became the 18th-century equivalent of a bestseller. The plight of the heroine, the dramatic tension, the evocation of atmosphere, not to mention the immediacy of the situation as described in the letters through Pamela's 'authentic' voice, all appealed to the large contingency of middle-class women readers who were both literate and leisured.

Fielding, extremely critical of 'writing for the moment', set out to **parody** this novel in *Shamela*, a skilful **burlesque** on the values and mannerisms of the first book of *Pamela*.

Here are the extracts. They each focus on an attempted rape by Mr B, assisted by a servant woman. In the extract from *Pamela*, Mr B has disguised himself as a maidservant.

Extract B from *Pamela*

At that the pretended She came to the Bed-side; and sitting down in a Chair, where the Curtain hid her, began to undress. Said I, Poor Mrs. *Ann*, I warrant your Head achs most sadly! How do you do? – She answer'd not one Word. Said the superlatively wicked Woman, You know I have order'd her not to answer you. And this Plot, to be sure, was laid, when she gave her those Orders, the Night before.

I heard her, as I thought, breathe all quick and short. Indeed, said I, Mrs. Jewkes, the poor Maid is not well. What ails you, Mrs *Ann*? And still no Answer was made.

But, I tremble to relate it, the pretended She came into Bed; but quiver'd like an Aspin-leaf; and I, poor Fool that I was! Pitied her much. – But well might the barbarous Deceiver tremble at his vile Dissimulation, and base Designs.

What Words shall I find, my dear Mother, (for my Father should not see this shocking Part) to describe the rest, and my Confusion, when the guilty Wretch took my Left-arm, and laid it under his Neck, as the vile Procuress held my Right; and then he clasp'd me round my Waist!

Said I, Is the Wench mad! Why, how now, Confidence! Thinking still it had been *Nan*. But he kissed me with frightful Vehemence; and then his Voice broke upon me like a Clap of Thunder. Now, *Pamela*, said he, is the dreadful Time of Reckoning come, that I have threaten'd. – I scream'd out in such a manner, as never any body heard the like. But there was nobody to help me; And both my Hands were secured, as I said. Sure never poor Soul was in such Agonies as I. Wicked Man! Said I; wicked, abominable Woman! O God! My God! This Time, this one Time! Deliver me from this Distress! Or strike me dead this Moment, and then I scream'd again and again.

Says he, One Word with you, *Pamela*; one Word hear me but; and hitherto you see I offer nothing to you. Is this nothing, said I, to be in Bed here? To hold my Hands between you? I will hear, if you will instantly leave the Bed, and take this villainous Woman from me!

Said she, (O Disgrace of Womankind!) What you do, Sir, do; don't stand dilly-dallying. She cannot exclaim worse than she has done. And she'll be quieter when she knows the worst.

Silence, said he to her; I must say one Word to you, *Pamela*; it is this: You see, now you are in my Power! – You cannot get from me, nor help yourself; Yet have I not offer'd any thing amiss to you. But if you resolve not to comply with my Proposals, I will not lose this Opportunity: If you do, I will not leave you.

O Sir, said I, leave me, leave me but, and I will do any thing I ought to do. – Swear then to me, said he, that you will accept my Proposals! – And then, (for this was all detestable Grimace) he put his Hand in my Bosom. With Struggling, Fright, Terror, I fainted away quite, and did not come to myself soon; so that they both, from the cold Sweats that I was in, thought me dying – And I remember no more than that, when, with great Difficulty, they brought me to myself, she was sitting on one side of the Bed, with her Cloaths on; and he on the other with his, and in his Gown and Slippers.

Extract C from *Shamela*

Thursday Night, Twelve o'Clock

Mrs. *Jervis* and I are just in Bed, and the Door unlocked; if my Master should come – Odsbobs! I hear him just coming in at the Door. You see I write in the present Tense, as Parson *Williams* says. Well, he is in Bed between us, we both shamming a Sleep, he steals his Hand into my Bosom, which I, as if in my Sleep, press close to me with mine, and then pretend to awake. – I no sooner see him, but I scream out to Mrs. *Jervis*, she feigns likewise but just to come to herself; we both begin, she to becall, and I to bescratch very liberally. After having made a pretty free Use of my Fingers, without any great Regard to the Parts I attack'd, I counterfeit a Swoon. Mrs. *Jervis* then cries out, O, Sir, what have you done, you have murthured poor *Pamela*; she is gone, she is gone. –

O what a Difficulty it is to keep one's Countenance, when a violent Laugh desires to burst forth.

The poor Booby frightened out of his Wits, jumped out of Bed, and in his Shirt, sat down by my Bed-side, pale and trembling, for the Moon shone, and I kept my Eyes wide open, and pretended to fix them in my Head. Mrs. *Jervis* apply'd Lavender Water, and Hartshorn, and this, for a full Half Hour; when thinking I had carried it on long enough, and being likewise unable to continue the Sport any longer, I began in Degrees to come to my self.

Questions

AO1: Developing an informed response to text

- What impressions do you have of Pamela and Shamela?
- What do you learn about their thoughts, feelings and attitudes to love?

AO2: Understanding how form, structure and language shape meaning

- Compare the ways the writers use:
  - the first-person viewpoint
  - dialogue
  - language.
- Compare the ways the reader responds to each passage.

AO3: Exploring connections, comparisons and the interpretations of other readers

- Compare the ways the passages present the attempted seduction.
- Richardson is trying to give his readers immediate access to Pamela's feelings through use of the letter form. How far do you agree with the view that it is a bogus immediacy which Fielding finds easy to satirise?
- Dr Johnson said that we 'know more of the human heart in one letter of Richardson's than in all of *Tom Jones*'. How far do you agree?

AO3: Understanding the significance and influence of contexts

- How are the two writers influenced by their contexts?
- What do you learn of the position of women in these extracts?
- What do you learn about attitudes to love in the extracts?

Further reading

Other works that you might want to dip into are *Clarissa* by Richardson – another epistolary novel, with its focus on the two lovers, Clarissa and Lovelace. Also Fielding's picaresque novel, *Joseph Andrews,* traces the adventures of Pamela's brother.

- *The Rise of the Novel* by Ian Watt (Pimlico)
- *The Eighteenth Century Novel*, ed. John Richetti (Cambridge)
- *The English Novel: An Introduction* by Terry Eagleton (Blackwell)
- *Shamela, Tom Jones, Joseph Andrews* by Henry Fielding
- *Pamela, Clarissa* by Samuel Richardson

Later 18th century

By the end of the century, the three-volume confessional novel was well established, as were both satirical and picaresque novels. Gothic novels and a good many romantic novels were popular with the largely female reading public.

Perhaps the most popular of these fictions was *Evelina*, a novel by Fanny Burney (1752–1840), published anonymously in 1778. The novel was written in epistolary form and was a love story, with its heroine rising above adversity to make a suitable marriage.

The passage we are going to look at, however, moves us off the main novel highway since it comes from a different genre. We have noted that the reading public was dominated by women; it is also true to say that many novels of the period represented female experience. Mary Wollstonecraft (1759–97) was critical of the contemporary sentimental novel, complaining of the 'unnatural delicacy of feeling that the herd of novelists glorified'. She is seen as a key figure in the feminist tradition by 20th- and 21st-century feminists, and we are going to consider her polemic, *A Vindication of the Rights of Women* (1792) which makes a plea for a fundamental change in society's perception of the function, place and potential of women. In this extract she addresses the topic of women and love. Note her reference to Lovelace from *Clarissa*.

Fig. 5.2 *Mary Wollstonecraft*

Extract D from *A Vindication of the Rights of Women*

But one great truth women have yet to learn, though much it imports them to act accordingly. In the choice of a husband, they should not be led astray by the qualities of a lover – for a lover the husband, even supposing him to be wise and virtuous, cannot long remain.

Were women more rationally educated, could they take a more comprehensive view of things, they would be contented to love but once in their lives; and after marriage calmly let passion subside into friendship – into that tender intimacy, which is the best refuge from care; yet is built on such pure, still affections, that idle jealousies would not be allowed to disturb the discharge of the sober duties of life, or to engross the thoughts that ought to be otherwise employed. This is a state in which many men live; but few, very few, women. And the difference may easily be accounted for, without recurring to a sexual character. Men, for whom we are told women were made, have too much occupied the thoughts of women; and this association has so entangled love with all their motives of action; and, to harp a little on an old string, having been solely employed either to prepare themselves to excite love, or actually putting their lessons in practice, they cannot live without love. But, when a sense of duty, or fear of shame, obliges them to restrain this pampered desire of pleasing beyond certain lengths, too far for delicacy, it is true, though far from criminality, they obstinately determine to love, I speak of the passion, their husbands to the end of the chapter – and then acting the part which they foolishly exacted from their lovers, they become abject wooers and fond slaves.

Men of wit and fancy are often rakes; and fancy is the food of love. Such men will inspire passion. Half the sex, in its present infantile state, would pine for a Lovelace; a man so witty, so graceful, and so valiant; and can they deserve blame for acting according to principles so constantly inculcated? They want a lover, and protector; and behold him kneeling before them – bravery prostrate to beauty! The virtues of a husband are thus thrown by love into the background, and gay hopes, or lively emotions, banish reflection till the day of reckoning come; and come it surely will, to turn the sprightly lover into a surly suspicious tyrant, who contemptuously insults the very weakness he fostered.

Questions

AO1: Developing an informed response to text

- Trace Wollstonecraft's train of thought in this passage.

AO2: Understanding how form, structure and language shape meaning

- How does the writer present her ideas? You should consider form, structure and language.

AO3: Exploring connections, comparisons and the interpretations of other readers

- Read the passage from Jill Tweedie's *In the Name of Love* which follows, then compare the ideas of the two women and the ways they present them.
- Go on to compare both these passages with other polemic that you have come across in your reading.
- How far do you agree with the view that Tweedie mounts the more convincing argument?

AO4: Understanding the significance and influence of contexts

- What do the two passages have to tell you about the position of women and attitudes to love in society?

Extract E from *In the Name of Love*

Love may turn out to be our only solace in this loneliness of a million million galaxies but we must learn to shift its source from the tempests of the limbic system to the cool places of the neo-cortex if it is to be a true solace and not a mirage that dissolves as we get close. The loves we know (late-comers though they are) are passion and romance and both, if given the centre of the stage, will not sustain the burden of reality. Indeed, both are an escape from reality. Romance cocoons itself in chiffon and lace, perfumes and songs and rose-coloured spectacles, to avoid any hint of the reality of the loved one that would melt the glittering bauble away. Passion puts all its energies to exaggerating reality, tightening emotional strings to the highest pitch in an all-consuming drive towards tension, drama, danger and death. Once, at its start, romance served an elegant purpose, it produced the first gentleness and reciprocity between the sexes, a brave enough attempt to supply by art what was missing in fact. Now it is past its peak and well on the way to decrepitude and romantic flourishes can be seen to have a devious purpose. Like the fine pomanders carried by seventeenth-century ladies to cover the effluvia of unwashed bodies and rotting teeth, it conveniently conceals the gangrenous patches in the relationships between the sexes, the reality of male oppression and female manipulation, the loveless and often brutal marriages and lovelessness itself ...

Thanks ever so, but no thank you. Love, used in a romantic or a passionate context, is merely a licence for indulgence of our own needs and fantasies, a prop for our weaknesses and an accessory for our shaky egos. True love is, above all, an emanation of reason, a rational apprehension of another human being and a logical assessment of his or her particular needs, virtues and failings, in the light of reality. In some ways women have already understood this better than men but our subordinate position and the resulting dependency and weak sense of self have prevented us acting on it. Which is the other and perhaps the greatest obstacle of all still to be overcome in the name of love.

Further reading

- *A Vindication of the Rights of Women* by Mary Wollstonecraft (Penguin Classics)
- *In the Name of Love* by Jill Tweedie (Jonathan Cape)
- *The Female Eunuch, The Whole Woman* by Germaine Greer (Doubleday)

Early 19th century

The Romantic period in English literature is generally agreed to have spanned 1775 to 1840. In much of the writing, the influence of the gothic can be traced in characters, events and settings, but the key characteristics of writing during this period are the worship of nature and the foregrounding of passion and imagination. Jane Austen (1775–1817) was born at the start of this literary era. She is recognised as the writer who brought the English novel to maturity, paving the way for developments in the 19th century. Each of her novels is about a small group of middle-class people in a limited – even limiting – environment. She shapes the apparently unimportant events of their lives into a comedy of manners. Her key concern is courtship and marriage. She creates comedy but also shows compassion. Beneath the **irony** is moral commentary.

Persuasion (1818) is her last completed novel. In this book she shows the established order as confining and outdated and creates a mature and independent heroine who frees herself from paternal authority. Anne Elliot had been persuaded by her family and an interfering friend to refuse Captain Wentworth eight and a half years previously, but she has never stopped loving him. Here is her second chance.

Extract F from *Persuasion*

She had only time, however, to move closer to the table where he had been writing, when footsteps were heard returning; the door opened, it was himself. He begged their pardon, but he had forgotten his gloves, was again out of the room, almost before Mrs Musgrove was aware of his being in it – the work of an instant!

The revolution which one instant had made in Anne was almost beyond expression. The letter, with a direction hardly legible, to 'Miss A. E.', was evidently the one which he had been folding so hastily. While supposed to be writing only to Captain Benwick, he had been also addressing her! On the contents of that letter depended all which this world could do for her! Anything was possible, anything might be defied rather than suspense. Mrs Musgrove had little arrangements of her own at her own table; to their protection she must trust, and sinking into the chair which he had occupied, succeeding to the very spot where he had leaned and written, her eyes devoured the following words: –

I can listen no longer in silence. I must speak to you by such means as are within my reach. You pierce my soul. I am half agony, half hope. Tell me not that I am too late, that such precious feelings are gone for ever. I offer myself to you again with a heart even more your own than when you almost broke it, eight years and a half ago. Dare not say that man forgets sooner than woman, that his love has an earlier death. I have loved none but you. Unjust I may have been, weak and resentful I have been, but never inconstant. You alone have brought me to Bath. For you alone I think and plan. Have you not seen this? Can you fail to have understood my wishes? I had not waited even these ten days, could I have read your feelings, as I think you must have penetrated mine. I can hardly write. I am every instant hearing something which overpowers me. You sink your voice, but I can distinguish the tones of that voice when they would be lost on others. Too good, too excellent creature! You do us justice, indeed. You do believe that there is true attachment and constancy among men. Believe it to be most fervent, most undeviating in

F.W.

I must go, uncertain of my fate; but I shall return hither, or follow your party, as soon as possible. A word, a look, will be enough to decide whether I enter your father's house this evening, or never.

Such a letter was not to be soon recovered from. Half an hour's solitude and reflection might have tranquillized her; but the ten minutes only, which now passed before she was interrupted, with all the restraints of her situation, could do nothing towards tranquillity. Every moment rather brought fresh agitation. It was an overpowering happiness. And before she was beyond the first stage of full sensation, Charles, Mary, and Henrietta, all came in.

The absolute necessity of seeming like herself produced then an immediate struggle; but after a while she could do no more. She began not to understand a word they said, and was obliged to plead indisposition and excuse herself. They could then see that she looked very ill – were shocked and concerned – and would not stir without her for the world. This was dreadful. Would they only have gone away, and left her in the quiet possession of that room, it would have been her cure; but to have them all standing or waiting around her was distracting, and, in desperation, she said she would go home.

'By all means, my dear,' cried Mrs Musgrove, 'go home directly, and take care of yourself, that you may be fit for the evening. I wish Sarah was here to doctor you, but I am no doctor myself. Charles, ring and order a chair. She must not walk.'

But the chair would never do. Worse than all! To lose the possibility of speaking two words to Captain Wentworth in the course of her quiet, solitary progress up the town (and she felt almost certain of meeting him) could not be borne. The chair was earnestly protested against; and Mrs Musgrove, who thought only of one sort of illness, having assured herself, with some anxiety, that there had been no fall in the case; that Anne had not, at anytime lately, slipped down, and got a blow on her head; that she was perfectly convinced of having had no fall; could part with her cheerfully, and depend on finding her better at night.

Anxious to omit no possible precaution, Anne struggled, and said –

'I am afraid, ma'am, that it is not perfectly understood. Pray be so good as to mention to the other gentlemen that we hope to see your whole party this evening. I am afraid there has been some mistake; and I wish you particularly to assure Captain Harville and Captain Wentworth that we hope to see them both.'

'Oh, my dear, it is quite understood, I give you my word. Captain Harville has no thought but of going.'

'Do you think so? But I am afraid; and I should be so very sorry. Will you promise me to mention it when you see them again? You will see them both again this morning, I daresay. Do promise me.'

'To be sure I will, if you wish it. Charles, if you see Captain Harville anywhere, remember to give Miss Anne's message. But, indeed, my dear, you need not be uneasy. Captain Harville holds himself quite engaged, I'll answer for it; and Captain Wentworth the same, I daresay.'

Anne could do no more; but her heart prophesied some mischance to damp the perfection of her felicity. It could not be very lasting, however. Even if he did not come to Camden Place himself, it would be in her power to send an intelligible sentence by Captain Harville.

Another momentary vexation occurred. Charles, in his real concern and good nature, would go home with her: there was no preventing him. This was almost cruel. But she could not long be ungrateful; he was sacrificing an engagement at a gunsmith's to be of use to her; and she set off with him, with no feeling but gratitude apparent.

They were in Union Street, when a quicker step behind, a something of familiar sound, gave her two moments' preparation for the sight of Captain Wentworth. He joined them; but, as if irresolute whether to join or to pass on, said nothing – only looked. Anne could command herself enough to receive that look, and not repulsively. The cheeks which had been pale now glowed, and the movements which had hesitated were decided. He walked by her side. Presently, struck by a sudden thought, Charles said –

'Captain Wentworth, which way are you going? Only to Gay Street, or farther up the town?'

'I hardly know,' replied Captain Wentworth, surprised.

'Are you going as high as Belmont? Are you going near Camden Place? Because, if you are, I shall have no scruple in asking you to take my place, and give Anne your arm to her father's door. She is rather done for this morning, and must not go so far without help; and I ought to be at that fellow's in the market place. He promised me the sight of a capital gun he is just going to send off; said he would keep it unpacked to the last possible moment, that I might see it; and if I do not turn back now, I have no chance. By his description, it is a good deal like the second-sized double-barrel of mine, which you shot with one day round Winthrop.'

There could not be an objection. There could only be a most proper alacrity, a most obliging compliance for public view; and smiles reined in and spirits dancing in private rapture. In half a minute, Charles was at the bottom of Union Street again, and the other two proceeding together; and soon words enough had passed between them to decide their direction towards the comparatively quiet and retired gravel walk, where the power of conversation would make the present hour a blessing indeed; and prepare it for all the immortality which the happiest recollections of their own future lives could bestow. There they exchanged again those feelings and those promises which had once before seemed to secure everything, but which had been followed by so many, many years of division and estrangement. There they returned again into the past, more exquisitely happy, perhaps, in their re-union, than when it had first been projected; more tender, more tried, more fixed in a knowledge of each other's character, truth, and attachment; more equal to act, more justified in acting. And there, as they slowly paced the gradual ascent, heedless of every group around them, seeing neither sauntering politicians, bustling housekeepers, flirting girls, nor nurserymaids and children, they could indulge in those retrospections and acknowledgments, and especially in those explanations of what had directly preceded the present moment, which were so poignant and so ceaseless in interest. All the little variations of the last week were gone through; and of yesterday and today there could scarcely be an end.

Questions

AO1: Developing an informed response to text
- What impressions have you formed of the characters of Anne and Captain Wentworth?
- What attitudes to love are shown here?

AO2: Understanding how form, structure and language shape meaning
- Explore the writer's use of narrative viewpoint and structure.
- Consider the appropriateness of the choices of language.

AO3: Exploring connections, comparisons and the interpretations of other readers
- Compare the presentation of love in this passage with the passages from *Tom Jones* and *Pamela*.
- It has been said that Jane Austen's strength in *Persuasion* is that she presents men and women as moral equals. How do you respond to this view?

AO4: Understanding the significance and influence of contexts
- Read the extract from Fay Weldon's *Letters to Alice* which follows, then comment on the ways Jane Austen uses the 19th-century context in her writing.

In her book *Letters to Alice*, Fay Weldon is writing to her fictional niece, a student of English Literature. Here are her comments on Jane Austen and her society.

Extract G from *Letters to Alice*

The novel form has developed through the centuries and requires a reader more or less as cultivated as the writer. He, or she, writes out of a society: links the past of that society with its future … Jane Austen concerned herself with what to us are observable truths, because we agree with them. They were not so observable at the time. We believe with her that Elizabeth should marry for love, … She believed it was better not to marry at all, than to marry without love. Such notions were quite new at the time. It surprises us that in her writing she appears to fail to take the pleasures of sex into account, but that was the convention at the time: we disapprove, where her society most approves. She is not a gentle writer. Do not be misled: she is not ignorant, merely discreet: not innocent, merely graceful … She struggled to perceive and describe the flow of beliefs that typified her time, and more, to suggest for the first time that the personal, the emotional, is in fact the moral – nowadays, of course, for good or bad, we argue that it is political. She left a legacy for the future to build upon.

Further reading

- *Pride and Prejudice, Sense and Sensibility, Emma, Northanger Abbey* by Jane Austen
- *Letters to Alice* by Fay Weldon (Coronet Books)

The later 19th and early 20th centuries

The Victorian/Edwardian era in literature began in 1840. The literature of this period reflects a continued interest in 'romantic' concerns such as the vulnerabilities of children, the countryside, and the expression of feelings. But more dominant in this time of the Empire are the themes of duty, trade, education and morality. Social and class divisions are clear; family values are stressed; and domesticity and the concept of the 'angel of the house' revered. The reading public continued to grow, enjoying the serialisation of long novels.

We start with Charlotte Brontë. If you read her letters, you will find that on her return from Belgium where she had been sent to learn French, she began a correspondence with a professor with whom she had fallen in love. He had been no more than impersonally kind to her, but back home she could not forget him. Her letters reveal her deep feelings. Such thoughts and feelings appear in her novel *Villette* (1854), an **autobiographical fiction** from where we take our next extract. In this novel, Lucy Snowe takes up a post as a teacher in a girls' school in Villette (Brussels). She has little French, beauty or money, but she proves to be a valuable and hard-working member of staff, appreciated by her headmistress, Mme Beck. She falls in love with a professor, Paul Emmanuel. When he leaves for a three-year stay in the West Indies at the end of the novel, he leaves Lucy in charge of his school and promises he will come back to her.

Extract H from *Villette*

The secret of my success did not lie so much in myself, in any endowment, any power of mine, as in a new state of circumstances, a wonderfully changed life, a relieved heart. The spring which moved my energies lay far away beyond seas, in an Indian isle. At parting, I had been left a legacy; such a thought for the present, such a hope for the future, such a motive for a persevering, a laborious, an enterprising, a patient and a brave course – I could not flag. Few

Fig. 5.3 The Kiss *by Gustav Klimt (1862–1918)*

Fig. 5.4 *Charlotte Brontë*

things shook me now; few things had importance to vex, intimidate, or depress me; most things pleased – mere trifles had a charm.

Do not think that this genial flame sustained itself, or lived wholly on a bequeathed hope or a parting promise. A generous provider supplied bounteous fuel. I was spared all chill, all stint; I was not suffered to fear penury; I was not tried with suspense. By every vessel he wrote; he wrote as he gave and as he loved, in full-handed, full-hearted plenitude. He wrote because he liked to write; he did not abridge, because he cared not to abridge. He sat down, he took pen and paper, because he loved Lucy and had much to say to her; because he was faithful and thoughtful, because he was tender and true. There was no sham and no cheat, and no hollow unreal in him. Apology never dropped her slippery oil on his lips – never proffered, by his pen, her coward feints and paltry nullities; he would give neither a stone, nor an excuse – neither a scorpion, nor a disappointment; his letters were real food that nourished, living water that refreshed.

And was I grateful? God knows! I believe that scarce a living being so remembered, so sustained, dealt with in kind so constant, honourable and noble, could be otherwise than grateful to the death.

Adherent to his own religion (in him was not the stuff of which is made the facile apostate), he freely left me my pure faith. He did not teaze or tempt. He said: –

'Remain a Protestant. My little English Puritan, I love Protestantism in you. I own its severe charm. There is something in its ritual I cannot receive myself, but it is the sole creed for "Lucy."' …

And now the three years are past: M. Emmanuel's return is fixed. It is Autumn; he is to be with me ere the mists of November come. My school flourishes, my house is ready: I have made him a little library, filled its shelves with the books he left in my care: I have cultivated out of love for him (I was naturally no florist) the plants he preferred, and some of them are yet in bloom. I thought I loved him when he went away; I love him now in another degree; he is more my own.

The sun passes the equinox; the days shorten, the leaves grow sere; but – he is coming.

The skies hang full and dark – a rack sails from the west; the clouds cast themselves into strange forms – arches and broad radiations; there rise resplendent mornings – glorious, royal, purple as monarch in his state; the heavens are one flame; so wild are they, they rival battle at its thickest – so bloody, they shame Victory in her pride. I know some signs of the sky; I have noted them ever since childhood. God, watch that sail! Oh! Guard it!

The wind shifts to the west. Peace, peace, Banshee – 'keening' at every window! It will rise – it will swell – it shrieks out long: wander as I may through the house this night, I cannot lull the blast. The advancing hours make it strong: by midnight, all sleepless watchers hear and fear a wild south-west storm.

That storm roared frenzied for seven days. It did not cease till the Atlantic was strewn with wrecks: it did not lull till the deeps had gorged their full sustenance. Not till the destroying angel of tempest had achieved his perfect work, would he fold the wings whose waft was thunder – the tremor of whose plumes was storm.

Peace, be still! Oh! A thousand weepers, praying in agony on waiting shores, listened for that voice, but it was not uttered – not uttered till, when the hush came, some could not feel it: till, when the sun returned, his light was night to some!

Here pause: pause at once. There is enough said. Trouble no quiet, kind heart; leave sunny imaginations hope. Let it be theirs to conceive the delight of joy born again fresh out of great terror, the rapture of rescue from peril, the wondrous reprieve from dread, the fruition of return. Let them picture union and a happy succeeding life.

■ Questions

AO1: Developing an informed response to text

■ What impressions have you formed of Lucy Snowe and Paul Emmanuel and of their relationship?

■ Explore Brontë's use of setting in the novel.

AO2: Understanding how form, structure and language shape meaning

■ Explore the ways Brontë uses language to present the situation to the reader.

■ Comment on the use of the first-person viewpoint.

■ What do you understand by and what is your response to the ending?

AO3: Exploring connections, comparisons and the interpretations of other readers

■ Compare the thoughts and feelings expressed in her letters with those presented in the novel.

■ What similarities and what differences do you observe between this portrayal of love and those in the extracts already studied?

■ In her time Charlotte Brontë was accused of being a strong-minded woman who wrote 'coarse' novels. How do you respond to this view?

AO4: Understanding the significance and influence of contexts

■ What does the extract tell you about the position of women in 19th-century England?

■ What do you learn about attitudes to love?

■ Further reading

■ *Jane Eyre, The Professor, Shirley* by Charlotte Brontë

■ *Wuthering Heights* by Emily Brontë

■ *Agnes Grey, The Tenant of Wildfell Hall* by Anne Brontë

■ *The Life of Charlotte Brontë* by Mrs Gaskell

■ *The Mill on the Floss, Middlemarch* by George Eliot

■ Activity

Review of the definition

Before we move on to the next extract, take some time to think about the extracts you have studied so far in this chapter, and re-visit the definitions of the novel that we discussed at the beginning.

■ Does Eagleton's definition apply to what you have read?

■ Does your reading support E. M. Forster's definition?

■ Do you agree with Golding's thoughts about endings in the light of your reading of the extract from *Villette*?

Charles Dickens

We now move on to consider a passage from *Great Expectations* (1860/61) by Charles Dickens (1812–70). The story is narrated in the first person but this time by the male voice of Pip. There are many representations of love in the novel – Pip's tortured relationship with Estella, or Miss Havisham the jilted bride, for example – but this extract has a more comic tone. Along with Bennett and Mrs Gaskell, Dickens is noted for the **social realism** of his novels. Pip visits his friend, the eccentric Wemmick, one of a gallery of minor characters. He is introduced to Miss Skiffins and to Wemmick's father, the Aged P, who reads to them from the newspaper.

Extract I from *Great Expectations* by Charles Dickens

The Aged's reading reminded me of the classes at Mr. Wopsle's great-aunt's, with the pleasanter peculiarity that is seemed to come through a keyhole. As he wanted the candles close to him, and as he was always on the verge of putting either his head or the newspaper into them, he required as much watching as a powder-mill. But Wemmick was equally untiring and gentle in his vigilance, and the Aged read on, quite unconscious of his many rescues. Whenever he looked at us, we all expressed the greatest interest and amazement, and nodded until he resumed again.

As Wemmick and Miss Skiffins sat side by side, and as I sat in a shadowy corner, I observed a slow and gradual elongation of Mr. Wemmick's mouth, powerfully suggestive of his slowly and gradually stealing his arm round Miss Skiffin's waist. In course of time I saw his hand appear on the other side of Miss Skiffin's; but at that moment Miss Skiffins neatly stopped him with the green glove, unwound his arm again as if it were an article of dress, and with the greatest deliberation laid it on the table before her. Miss Skiffins's composure while she did this was one of the most remarkable sights I have ever seen, and if I could have thought the act consistent with abstraction of mind, I should have deemed that Miss Skiffins performed it mechanically.

By-and-bye, I noticed Wemmick's arm beginning to disappear again, and gradually fading out of view. Shortly afterwards, his mouth began to widen again. After an interval of suspense on my part that was quite enthralling and almost painful, I saw his hand appear on the other side of Miss Skiffins. Instantly, Miss Skiffins stopped it with the neatness of a placid boxer, took off that girdle or cestus as before, and laid it on the table. Taking the Table to represent the path of virtue, I am justified in stating that during the whole time of the Aged's reading, Wemmick's arm was straying from the path of virtue and being recalled to it by Miss Skiffins.

At last the Aged read himself into a light slumber. This was the time for Wemmick to produce a little kettle, a tray of glasses, and a black bottle with a porcelain-topped cork, representing some clerical dignitary of a rubicund and social aspect. With the aid of these appliances we all had something warm to drink: including the Aged, who was soon awake; of course I knew better than to offer to see Miss Skiffins home, and under the circumstances I thought I had best go first: which I did, taking a cordial leave of the Aged, and having passed a pleasant evening.

Questions

AO1: Developing an informed response to the text

■ Describe your impressions of the events, the characters and the setting in the extract.

AO2: Understanding how form, structure and language shape meaning

■ How does Dickens present the relationship between Wemmick and Miss Skiffins?

■ How does he create humour?

AO3: Exploring connections, comparisons and the interpretations of other readers

■ Think back to the extract from *Tom Jones* and compare attitudes to love and the ways the two writers present them in the two extracts.

■ Compare the courtship ritual with any other account of courtship you have come across in your wider reading.

■ How do you react to the view that Dickens is little more than an 'entertainer'?

AO4: Understanding the significance and influence of contexts

■ What does this extract have to tell us about 19th-century attitudes to love and courtship?

Thomas Hardy

We turn now to an extract from *Far from the Madding Crowd* (1874) by Thomas Hardy (1840–1928). Hardy's novels depict in detail the rural world he knew as a child. He clearly loves the countryside, but has an unsentimental, realistic approach to it. Strong female characters are at the heart of his fiction. In this extract, Bathsheba has received a letter from Gabriel announcing that he is leaving. Realising how dependent she is on him, and that she has feelings for him, she goes to see him.

Extract J from *Far from the Madding Crowd* by Thomas Hardy

'You'll think it strange that I have come, but –'

'O no; not at all.'

'But I thought – Gabriel, I have been uneasy in the belief that I have offended you, and that you are going away on that account. It grieved me very much, and I couldn't help coming.'

'Offended me! As if you could do that, Bathsheba!'

'Haven't I?' she asked, gladly. 'But, what are you going away for else?'

'I am not going to emigrate, you know; I wasn't aware that you would wish me not to when I told 'ee, or I shouldn't have thought of doing it,' he said, simply. 'I have arranged for Little Weatherbury Farm, and shall have it in my own hands at Lady-Day. You know I've had a share in it for some time. Still, that wouldn't prevent my attending to your business as before, hadn't it been that things have been said about us.'

'What?' said Bathsheba, in surprise. 'Things said about you and me! What are they?'

'I cannot tell you.'

'It would be wiser if you were to, I think. You have played the part of mentor to me many times, and I don't see why you should fear to do it now.'

'It is nothing that you have done, this time. The top and tail o't is this – that I am sniffing about here, and waiting for poor Boldwood's farm, with a thought of getting you some day.'

'Getting me! What does that mean?'

'Marrying o' 'ee, in plain British. You asked me to tell, so you mustn't blame me.'

Bathsheba did not look quite so alarmed as if a cannon had been discharged by her ear, which was what Oak had expected. 'Marrying me! I didn't know it was that you meant,' she said, quietly. 'Such a thing as that is too absurd – too soon – to think of, by far!'

'Yes; of course, it is too absurd. I don't desire any such thing; I should think that was plain enough by this time. Surely, surely you be the last person in the world I think of marrying. It is too absurd, as you say.'

'"Too – s-s-soon" were the words I used.'

'I must beg your pardon for correcting you, but you said "too absurd," and so do I.'

'I beg your pardon too!' she returned, with tears in her eyes. '"Too soon" was what I said. But it doesn't matter a bit – not at all – but I only meant, "too soon." Indeed, I didn't, Mr. Oak, and you must believe me!'

Gabriel looked her long in the face, but the firelight being faint there was not much to be seen. 'Bathsheba,' he said, tenderly and in surprise, and coming closer: 'if I only knew one thing – whether you would allow me to love you and win you, and marry you after all – if only I knew that!'

'But you will never know,' she murmured.

'Why?'

'Because you never ask.'

'Oh – Oh!' said Gabriel, with a low laugh of joyousness. 'My own dear –'

'You ought not to have sent me that harsh letter this morning,' she interrupted, 'it shows you didn't care a bit about me, and were ready to desert me like all the rest of them! It was very cruel of you, considering I was the first sweetheart that you ever had, and you were the first I ever had; and I shall not forget it!'

'Now, Bathsheba, was ever anybody so provoking?' he said, laughing. 'You know it was purely that I, as an unmarried man, carrying on a business for you as a very taking young woman, had a proper hard part to play – more particular that people knew I had a sort of feeling for 'ee; and I fancied, from the way we were mentioned together, that it might injure your good name. Nobody knows the heat and fret I have been cause by it.'

'And was that all?'

'All.'

'Oh, how glad I am I came!' she exclaimed, thankfully, as she rose from her seat. 'I have thought so much more of you since I fancied you did not want even to see me again. But I must be going now, or I shall be missed. Why, Gabriel,' she said, with a slight laugh, as they went to the door, 'it seems exactly as if I had come courting you – how dreadful!'

'And quite right, too,' said Oak. 'I've danced at your skittish heels, my beautiful Bathsheba, for many a long mile, and many a long day; and it is hard to begrudge me this one visit.'

He accompanied her up the hill, explaining to her the details of his forthcoming tenure of the other farm. They spoke very little of their mutual feelings; pretty phrases and warm expressions being probably unnecessary between such tried friends. Theirs was that substantial affection which arises (if any arises at all) when the two who are thrown together begin first by knowing the rougher sides of each other's character, and not the best till further on, the romance growing up in the interstices of a mass of hard prosaic reality. This good-fellowship – camaraderie – usually occurring through similarity of pursuits, is unfortunately seldom superadded to love between the sexes, because men and women associate, not in their labours, but in their pleasures merely. Where, however, happy circumstance permits its development, the compounded feeling proves itself to be the only love which is strong as death – that love which many waters cannot quench, nor the floods drown, beside which the passion usually called by the name is evanescent as steam.

Fig. 5.5 *Still from a film of* **Far from the Madding Crowd**, *showing Bathsheba and Oak*

Questions

AO1: Developing an informed response to the text

- What does the passage tell you about the thoughts and feelings of the characters?

AO2: Understanding how form, structure and language shape meaning

- Explore the ways Hardy uses dialogue to communicate the thoughts and feelings of the characters.
- Comment on the narrative viewpoint.

AO3: Exploring connections, comparisons and the interpretations of other readers

- Compare the presentation of love and courtship in this extract with those in the Dickens and the Austen extracts.
- What do you make of the view that the power of this extract lies in the exploration of differences in gender and class?

AO4: Understanding the significance and influence of contexts

- Consider the ways this extract reflects late nineteenth-century attitudes to relationships between men and women.

Kate Chopin: a short story

We now take a second short detour from consideration of the novel as we look at a **short story** by Kate Chopin (1851–1904). Her collections of short stories present the reader with the clashing values of sex, love, class and race in Louisiana society. A strong theme running throughout her work is that of women's oppression and the suppression of self. Her short story *The Story of an Hour* (1894) is here reproduced in full; it explores what women might do in the absence of their husbands' and society's oppressive expectations.

Extract K *The Story of an Hour*

Knowing that Mrs Mallard was afflicted with a heart trouble, great care was taken to break to her as gently as possible the news of her husband's death.

It was her sister Josephine who told her, in broken sentences; veiled hints that revealed in half concealing. Her husband's friend Richards was there, too, near her. It was he who had been in the newspaper office when intelligence of the railroad disaster was received, with Brently Mallard's name leading the list of 'killed'. He had only taken the time to assure himself of its truth by a second telegram, and had hastened to forestall any less careful, less tender friend in bearing the sad message.

She did not hear the story as many women have heard the same, with a paralysed inability to accept its significance. She wept at once, with sudden, wild abandonment, in her sister's arms. When the storm of grief had spent itself she went away to her room alone. She would have no one follow her.

There stood, facing the open window, a comfortable, roomy armchair. Into this she sank, pressed down by a physical exhaustion that haunted her body and seemed to reach into her soul.

She could see in the open square before her house the tops of trees that were all aquiver with the new spring life. The delicious breath of rain was in the air. In the street below a peddler was crying his wares. The notes of a distant song which someone was singing reached her faintly, and countless sparrows were twittering in the eaves.

There were patches of blue sky showing here and there through the clouds that had met and piled one above the other in the west facing her window.

She sat with her head thrown back upon the cushion of the chair, quite motionless, except when a sob came up into her throat and shook her, as a child who has cried itself to sleep continues to sob in its dreams.

She was young, with a fair, calm face, whose lines bespoke repression and even a certain strength. But now there was a dull stare in her eyes, whose gaze was fixed away off yonder on one of those patches of blue sky. It was not a glance of reflection, but rather indicated a suspension of intelligent thought.

There was something coming to her and she was waiting for it, fearfully. What was it? She did not know; it was too subtle and elusive to name. But she felt it, creeping out of the sky, reaching toward her through the sounds, the scents, the colour that filled the air.

Now her bosom rose and fell tumultuously. She was beginning to recognise this thing that was approaching to possess her, and she was striving to beat it back with her will – as powerless as her two white slender hands would have been.

When she abandoned herself a little whispered word escaped her slightly parted lips. She said it over and over under her breath: 'free, free, free!' The vacant stare and the look of terror that had followed it went from her eyes. They stayed keen and bright. Her pulses beat fast, and the coursing blood warmed and relaxed every inch of her body.

She did not stop to ask if it were or were not a monstrous joy that held her. A clear and exalted perception enabled her to dismiss the suggestion as trivial.

She knew that she would weep again when she saw the kind, tender hands folded in death; the face that had never looked save with love upon her, fixed and grey and dead. But she saw beyond that bitter moment a long procession of years to come that would belong to her absolutely. And she opened and spread her arms out to them in welcome.

There would be no one to live for her during those coming years; she would live for herself. There would be no powerful will bending hers in that blind persistence with which men and women believe they have a right to impose a private will upon a fellow-creature. A kind intention or a cruel intention made the act seem no less a crime as she looked upon it in that brief moment of illumination.

And yet she had loved him – sometimes. Often she had not. What did it matter! What could love, the unsolved mystery, count for in face of this possession of self-assertion which she suddenly recognised as the strongest impulse of her being!

'Free! Body and soul free!' she kept whispering.

Josephine was kneeling before the closed door with her lips to the keyhole, imploring for admission. 'Louise, open the door! I beg; open the door – you will make yourself ill. What are you doing, Louise? For heaven's sake open the door.'

'Go away. I am not making myself ill.' No; she was drinking in a very elixir of life through that open window.

Her fancy was running riot along those days ahead of her. Spring days, and summer days, and all sorts of days that would be her own. She breathed a quick prayer that life might be long. It was only yesterday she had thought with a shudder that life might be long.

She arose at length and opened the door to her sister's importunities. There was a feverish triumph in her eyes, and she carried herself unwittingly like a goddess of Victory. She clasped her sister's waist, and together they descended the stairs. Richards stood waiting for them at the bottom.

Someone was opening the front door with a latchkey. It was Brently Mallard who entered, a little travel-stained, composedly carrying his grip-sack and umbrella. He had been far from the scene of the accident, and did not even know there had been one. He stood amazed at Josephine's piercing cry; at Richards' quick motion to screen him from the view of his wife.

But Richards was too late.

When the doctors came they said she had died of heart disease – of joy that kills.

Questions

AO1: Developing an informed response to the text
- Describe what happens in this story.
- How do you respond to Mrs Mallard's situation?

AO2: Understanding how form, structure and language shape meaning
- Explore the ways Chopin structures the story and the effects she achieves.
- What features of language enable Chopin to create the characters and the situation effectively? Note particularly the way she uses the weather.

AO3: Exploring connections, comparisons and the interpretations of other readers
- Read *The Yellow Wallpaper* by Charlotte Perkins Gilman (1860–1935) and compare the subject matter and the treatment of the female experience of love in the two stories.
- Compare the female experience of love in this story with all your wider reading.
- How do you respond to the criticism that this story is too contrived to be effective?

AO4: Understanding the significance and influence of contexts
- What does this story have to tell you about 19th-century attitudes to women and marriage?

Further reading
- *The Awakening* by Kate Chopin
- *The Yellow Wallpaper* by Charlotte Gilman Perkins

Moving forward in time, other notable collections of short stories are:
- *The Bloody Chamber* by Angela Carter
- *Bluebeard's Egg* by Margaret Atwood (look especially at the story *Hurricane Hazel* and the portrayal of romance)
- *Such Devoted Sisters* edited by Shena Mackay

🔍 The first half of the 20th century

In the **modernist** period, one of the results of the influence of the upheaval of World War One was a preoccupation with social and personal identity and the emergence of the psychological novel. The workings of the subconscious mind are explored and often **connotation** and association replace traditional narrative structures.

You will also find the **stream of consciousness** method in the novels of Virginia Woolf. She wrote *To the Lighthouse* in 1925 and it was published in 1927. In this novel, Woolf is trying to re-create her parents' marriage. The Ramsay family and guests are on holiday on the Isle of Skye in Scotland. The following extract is taken from Part One of the novel which describes the comings and goings of the group. The main focus is on Mrs Ramsay and on her relationship with her son, James, and her husband. Mr Ramsay is a philosopher in his sixties; Mrs Ramsay is fifty and renowned for her beauty; James is six.

This extract provides a snapshot of the Ramsays' relationship. Mrs Ramsay is reading a story to James as her husband, feeling threatened by a sense of failure, comes to her for reassurance and comfort. She soothes him. James feels neglected and angry. She is left exhausted, emptied and ill at ease since she knows her reassurance is based on exaggeration and half-truths.

Extract L from *To the Lighthouse* by Virginia Woolf

He was a failure, he repeated. Well, look then, feel then. Flashing her needles, glancing round about her, out of the window, into the room, at James himself, she assured him, beyond a shadow of a doubt, by her laugh, her poise, her competence (as a nurse carrying a light across a dark room assures a fractious child), that it was real; the house was full; the garden blowing. If he put implicit faith in her, nothing should hurt him; however deep he buried himself or climbed high, not for a second should he find himself without her. So boasting of her capacity to surround and protect, there was scarcely a shell of herself left for her to know herself by; all was so lavished and spent; and James, as he stood stiff between her knees, felt her rise in a rosy-flowered fruit tree laid with leaves and dancing boughs into which the beak of brass, the arid scimitar of his father, the egotistical man, plunged and smote, demanding sympathy.

Filled with her words, like a child who drops off satisfied, he said, at last, looking at her with humble gratitude, restored, renewed, that he would take a turn; he would watch the children playing cricket. He went.

Immediately, Mrs Ramsay seemed to fold herself together, one petal closed in another, and the whole fabric fell in exhaustion upon itself, so that she had only strength enough to move her finger, in exquisite abandonment to exhaustion, across the page of Grimm's fairy story, while there throbbed through her, like the pulse in a spring which has expanded to its full width and now gently ceases to beat, the rapture of successful creation.

Every throb of this pulse seemed, as he walked away to enclose her and her husband, and to give to each that solace which two different notes, one high, one low, struck together, seem to give each other as they combine. Yet, as the resonance died, and she turned to the fairy tale again, Mrs Ramsay felt not only exhausted

Activity

■ Consider the ways Woolf is using the stream of consciousness method here.

■ The stream of consciousness method had already been used by James Joyce in his novel *Ulysses* in an effort to capture the flux, development and complexity of an individual. Dip into this novel. Look especially at Molly Bloom's soliloquy at the end of the novel.

■ How might this kind of writing affect our definition of the novel and our opinions about endings?

Further reading

You will find the 'stream of consciousness' method in the novels of Virginia Woolf and James Joyce.

More traditional twentieth century narratives that you might want to explore are:

- *A Passage to India, Howard's End, A Room with a View* by E. M. Forster (1879–1970)
- *The Age of Innocence* by Edith Wharton (1862–1937)
- *The End of the Affair, The Heart of the Matter* by Graham Greene (1904–91)
- *The Go-Between* by L. P. Hartley (1895–1972)
- *The Sandcastle, The Bell* by Iris Murdoch (1919–99)
- *The Great Gatsby, Tender is the Night* by Scott Fitzgerald (1896–1940)

in body (afterwards, not at the time, she always felt this) but also there tinged her physical fatigue some faintly disagreeable sensation with another origin. Not that, as she read aloud the story of the Fisherman's Wife, she knew precisely what it came from; nor did she let herself put into words her dissatisfaction when she realised, at the turn of the page when she stopped and heard dully, ominously, a wave fall, how it came from this: she did not like, even for a second, to feel finer than her husband; and further, could not bear not being entirely sure, when she spoke to him, of the truth of what she said. Universities and people wanting him, lectures and books and their being of the highest importance – all that she did not doubt for a moment; but it was their relation, and his coming to her like that, openly, so that anyone could see, that discomposed her; for then people said he depended on her, when they must know that of the two he was infinitely the more important, and what she gave the world, in comparison with what he gave, negligible. But then again, it was the other thing too – not being able to tell him the truth, being afraid, for instance, about the greenhouse roof and the expense it would be, fifty pounds perhaps, to mend it; and then about his books, to be afraid that he might guess, what she a little suspected, that his last book was not quite his best book (she gathered that from William Bankes): and then to hide small daily things, and the children seeing it, and the burden it laid on them – all this diminished the entire joy, the pure joy, of the two notes sounding together, and let the sound die on her ear now with a dismal flatness.

The second half of the 20th century

Modernism gives way to **post-modernism** in the second half of the century. Post-modern writers tend to reject and mock the traditional linear and mimetic narrative, choosing to emphasise the artifice of the writing through a delight in games and verbal fireworks. Often there is no comfort of closure, but randomness, discontinuity, ambivalence and paradox are key features of the writing. Genres and styles are often mixed; the work may belong to a recognisable genre but may be a mix of several. In order to study and understand a modern novel you will certainly need to become an **active** not a **passive** reader.

Revising the definition

Novelists in the early 21st century continue to try to define the novel. For example, Margaret Atwood says a novel 'is about somebody moving through time' and Carol Shields claims that 'a novel … is a story about the destiny of a child'.

Think about the modern novels you have read and make notes on how they might fit these definitions.

We have assembled a list of key words and terms that will help you to think about the modern novel:

- Fragmentary form, eclectic and collaged
- Cross-genre and multi-genre
- Addressing issues of style and form
- Considering varieties of forms of language
- Using stories within stories
- Unreliable narrator

- Variety of narrators
- Concerned with perception and point of view
- Questioning received ideas and the notion of 'truth'
- Cross-cultural
- Allusive
- Playing with – and concerned with issues about – time
- Exploring – re-writing and questioning – history
- Including some kind of social commentary or criticism
- Looking at themes to do with memory, identity and community
- Open endings
- Multiple endings
- Making the reader work.

You may already be familiar with the work of post-modern novelists such as Angela Carter and Margaret Atwood. For our next extract we turn to *The Passion* by Jeanette Winterson (1987). Winterson is an experimental writer preoccupied with language; in this book she uses history as a means of creating a space where the reader is freed from all assumptions about narrative, character and linear time. Her book is structured in four parts: Part One tells the story of Henri with the Emperor Napoleon; Part Two is the story of Villanelle in Venice; Part Three is set in Russia where Henri and Villanelle meet; and Part Four switches and intertwines. In this extract, Villanelle, a gambler and a boatman's daughter from Venice with webbed feet, arrives at the house of the woman she loves.

Extract M from *The Passion* by Jeanette Winterson

She greeted me like an old friend and asked me straight away about the uniform.

'You're not a soldier.'

'It's fancy dress.'

I began to feel like Sarpi, that Venetian priest and diplomat, who said he never told a lie but didn't tell the truth to everyone. Many times that evening as we ate and drank and played dice I prepared to explain. But my tongue thickened and my heart rose up in self-defence.

'Feet,' she said.

'What?'

'Let me stroke your feet.'

Sweet Madonna, not my feet.

'I never take off my boots away from home. It's a nervous habit.'

'Then take off your shirt instead.'

Not my shirt, if I raised my shirt she'd find my breasts.

'In this inhospitable weather it would not be wise. Everyone has catarrh. Think of the fog.'

I saw her eyes stray lower. Did she expect my desire to be obvious?

What could I allow; my knees?

Instead I leaned forward and began to kiss her neck. She buried my head in her hair and I became her creature. Her smell, my atmosphere, and later when I was alone I cursed my nostrils for breathing the everyday air and emptying my body of her.

As I was leaving she said, 'My husband returns tomorrow.'

Oh.

As I was leaving she said, 'I don't know when I will see you again.'

Does she do this often? Does she walk the streets, when her husband goes away, looking for someone like me? Everyone in Venice has their weakness and their vice. Perhaps not only in Venice. Does she invite them to supper and hold them with her eyes and explain, a little sadly, that she can't make love? Perhaps this is her passion. Passion out of passion's obstacles. And me? Every game threatens a wild card. The unpredictable, the out of control. Even with a steady hand and a crystal ball we couldn't rule the world the way we wanted it. There are storms at sea and there are other storms inland. Only the convent windows look serenely out on both.

I went back to her house and banged on the door. She opened it a little. She looked surprised.

'I'm a woman,' I said, lifting up my shirt and risking the catarrh.

She smiled. 'I know.'

I didn't go home. I stayed.

■ Questions

AO1: Developing an informed response to the text
- Describe the characters and the events in this extract.
- What thoughts and feelings are described?

AO2: Understanding how form, structure and language shape meaning
- Explore the ways Winterson uses dialogue in the extract.
- What do you notice about the kinds of language she uses to express the thoughts and feelings?
- Comment on the mixture of the fantastic and the everyday.

AO3: Exploring connections, comparisons and the interpretations of other readers
- Compare this extract with the Dickens and Hardy extracts in terms of subject matter and style.
- Compare this extract with other descriptions of lesbian love from your reading.
- Winterson says 'I liked the idea of setting an intensely personal story against a brutal impersonal background'. How do you respond to this view?

AO4: Understanding the significance and influence of contexts
- Winterson herself says of the book: 'I wrote *The Passion* in 1986, boom-time of the Thatcher years, clock-race of yuppies and City boys, rich-quick, never count the cost. My own cities were invented; cities of language, cities of connection, words as gang-ways and bridges to the cities of the interior where the coin was not money, where it was emotion'. How do you respond to this assessment of her book?

The 21st century

We have chosen to end this chapter with an extract from Ian McEwan's *Atonement* (2001). The choice seems appropriate since it brings together so many of the ingredients of the novel that we have considered in this chapter. McEwan said that he wanted to write a love story (there are also elements of a whodunit or a war story) distanced from the present day. He calls this his Jane Austen novel. He claims that he was struck by the muted eroticism of Jane Austen's novels, by the dynamic created by what was *not* said or done. The cross-class affair between Robbie and Cecilia is the central love story; but the intervention of Cecilia's young sister, Briony, who claims to have witnessed a rape, wrecks the relationship. She spends the rest of her life trying to 'atone'.

If we turn to the extract, we see the two lovers moving from friendship to a different kind of relationship. We are apparently reading a traditional linear novel with an omniscient narrator.

Extract N from *Atonement* by Ian McEwan

Why was she crying? How could she begin to tell him when so much emotion, so many emotions, simply engulfed her? He in turn felt that his question was unfair, inappropriate, and he struggled to think of a way of putting it right. They stared at each other in confusion, unable to speak, sensing that something delicately established might slip from them. That they were old friends who had shared a childhood was now a barrier – they were embarrassed before their former selves. Their friendship had become vague and even constrained in recent years, but it was still an old habit, and to break it now in order to become strangers on intimate terms required a clarity of purpose which had temporarily deserted them. For the moment, there seemed no way out with words.

He put his hands on her shoulders, and her bare skin was cool to the touch. As their faces drew closer he was uncertain enough to think she might spring away, or hit him, movie-style, across the cheek with her open hand. Her mouth tasted of lipstick and salt. They drew away for a second, he put his arms around her and they kissed again with greater confidence. Daringly, they touched the tips of their tongues, and it was then she made the falling, sighing sound which, he realised later, marked a transformation.

Fig. 5.6 *Still from the film* **Atonement**

But this is McEwan, post-modern novelist. First we need to note the deliberate **intertextuality** – Cecilia is reading *Clarissa*, an epistolary novel with multiple viewpoints. Clarissa's sister is Arabella, the name of the heroine of the play Briony is writing. And it is a love letter that leads to Robbie's downfall. As in many post-modern novels, there is a strong, overt interest in how fiction is constructed. In this four-part novel, the first three parts appear to come from a traditional narrative with an omniscient narrator: Part One paints a picture of the life of one upper-class family before World War Two; Part Two describes Robbie's return from Dunkirk; Part Three is set in London where both Cecilia and Briony are working as nurses. However, the traditional narrative is undermined when, in Part Three, Briony receives a rejection notice for a novel she has submitted. It comes with advice and a suggested revised synopsis of the novel. That synopsis becomes the novel we are reading. Part Four introduces Briony the writer in old age (1999), reflecting on her writing. So it is that twists of perspective and structure reveal that Parts One, Two, and Three are a novel within a novel. And the ending leaves us wondering and with a sense of unease – yet another post-modern feature!

Time to revise your definition of the novel again.

💡 *Summary*

A chapter cannot do justice to the required breadth and depth of your wider reading, but we hope this chapter has provided a launching pad for your own discoveries.

Working through the extracts in this chapter will give you an overview of how the theme of **love** has been represented through time.

We have focused on:

- some major novelists, literary traditions and individual writing styles
- ways of linking extracts within and across different periods
- the development of the skills of close reading, analysis and interpretation.

Drama about love

Aims of the chapter:

- introduces wider reading of drama about love, tracing the development of the genre from Shakespeare to the present day

- develops awareness of playwrights' uses of form, structure and language

- provides examples for further study of playwrights' subject matter and styles, encouraging links and connections with other plays, and with poetry and prose texts

- shows how the Assessment Objectives can be applied to your reading

- continues the study of drama in its literary, historical and cultural contexts.

Introduction

In this chapter you will be looking at plays written and performed from the 16th century onwards, focusing on drama from England, Ireland, Europe and America. The aim is to indicate key developments in drama from Shakespeare onwards, always keeping in mind the ways the playwrights present aspects of love and human relationships. The extracts will introduce you to examples of:

- tragedy
- comedy
- Restoration comedy
- realism
- epic theatre
- minimalism
- modern drama.

The extracts are printed in chronological order. In some periods – the 16th century, for example – drama is a dominant genre, but in the 19th century, as far as canonical texts are concerned, English drama tends to give way to prose or poetry. The extracts provide opportunities for close reading, but we hope that they will also act as 'tasters' to encourage you to read the whole plays from which they are taken. All the plays are by men, but all of them except *Bent* foreground women as key characters, and explore women's roles in relationships and in society. As you work through this book you should consider the possible reasons for the dominance of male dramatists, and do some research into the contributions that women have made to 20th- and 21st-century theatre as playwrights, directors and actors.

At AS you have already studied some drama texts within your chosen option. You will find the sections on drama in the Nelson Thornes *AQA English Literature for AS* Student Books: *Victorian Literature, Literature of World War One* and *The Struggle for Identity in Modern Literature* very useful. The chapters on writing about drama for coursework, and on wider reading in drama, give you plenty of relevant contextual information about major playwrights and their plays from the 19th century onwards.

Your reading log

It is important, as you work through this chapter, to keep a log of the texts that you study as part of your wider reading in drama. Not only will this help you to trace the development of the genre through the ages, but your reading log will become a valuable revision tool for the examination. Whether you use the online resources, an electronic log you have created yourself or a paper file, is up to you, but you need to have a method that will enable you to keep a log of your reading which records both **genre** and **time**. The **English Literature through time** grid on pp124–5 is also there to help you.

As you study the extracts that follow, we have provided questions to help you, but for a fuller analytical study of an extract, remember to use the questions we gave you in Chapter 1.

Link

To remind yourself of the list of questions for analysing a text, turn back to pp5–6.

Link

For more information on the wider reading portfolio, see Chapter 1.

Don't forget to also keep your **wider reading portfolio** up to date.

Seeing live theatre and reading plays

Reading poetry and prose is largely something readers do on their own. Interaction about a text with other readers usually comes later, and need not come at all. Even watching a film or DVD can be a solitary activity, but live theatre creates a relationship between the actors who perform the text, and the audience who respond to their performance. As a member of the audience you are an essential part of what makes drama.

Literature reflects human relationships and situations, and people's thoughts and feelings and attitudes and values, in a variety of ways. Drama does this in a significantly different way from prose, especially prose fiction, in its handling of point of view. The dramatist shows characters acting out their conflicting emotions, ideas, attitudes and opinions. A script is the basic written record of these, out of which the director and the actors will build the whole play, through close reading and interpretation of the text, and the director's liaison with the designers of the set, lighting, costume, music and other effects. Drama also asks for responses from the audience: it expects our 'willing suspension of disbelief' as we watch the action unfold on stage, and at the same time demands that we make our own independent judgements of the characters' behaviour and attitudes as we see them develop in the course of the play.

Reading and rereading

You can read a whole play in much less time than a novel, but a play script demands an active and imaginative reader who can:

- lift the words off the page and follow the plot
- visualise the setting and effects
- understand the interactions of the characters and their motivations
- hear the tones in which they speak
- keep track of exits and entrances, and the roles of silent but visible characters.

Rereading any literary text is essential to deepen your knowledge and understanding. With drama, **rereading** has the additional sense of 'making a new reading'. In the theatre we don't have to seek out 'other readers' interpretations' of the text – we come face to face with them in action. This is why we can see the same play over and over again in different productions, and keep finding new interpretations of it.

Wider reading and the final examination

It can be difficult on your own to develop the skills listed above which you will need in order to respond successfully to a drama text. To practise these and prepare for the examination:

- do some of your wider reading of plays with other people so that you can all be involved in the process of bringing the script to life
- keep a log of your wider reading in drama, in a format that allows you to link texts across subject matter, periods and genres

Link

Use the Checklist for your study of drama texts on pp111–12 to develop your own agenda for reading and writing about plays.

- practise writing about a drama text as a play; as well as reading the language of the script closely, you should also think about the playwright's use of form and structure, and use of settings
- see as many plays from different **periods** as you can, on film or DVD if you cannot see them in the theatre
- see as many different **productions** of a play, or performances of a key role, as you can
- do some further research into the kind of theatre in which a pre-20th-century play would have first been performed, and the costumes of the period.

Drama through the ages, from the 16th century to the present day

Starting the study of drama with the 16th century obviously does not mean that drama did not exist before Shakespeare. Its origins go back to Ancient Greece and Rome, where drama developed out of religious rituals and secular festivals, and the two main strands of **tragedy** and **comedy** were established: tragedy through the Greek plays of Aeschylus, Sophocles and Euripides in the 5th and 6th centuries BC, and comedy through those of Aristophanes and later through the Roman writers, Plautus and Terence. In England the medieval **mystery plays** told stories from the Old and New Testaments in English, acted on moveable stages, called **pageants**, at fixed points in town streets. The familiar subject matter and language, the staging and performances which mixed serious religious teaching with down-to-earth comic scenes, brought live theatre to the whole community.

Fig. 6.1 *A pageant cart*

The second half of the 16th century and the first half of the 17th, between 1585 and 1642, was a great period for English drama, particularly tragedy. Since the time of the Ancient Greeks, tragedy has always been concerned with the inevitability of human suffering, and comedy with the absurd ways in which people behave. The Greek philosopher Aristotle (384–322 BC) defined tragedy as being about an important person whose fall from his high position (and the focus of the tragedy almost always was a man) is caused by a fatal flaw in his character. Comedy, according to Aristotle, is about recognisably ordinary people, whose faults cause ridiculous situations. We still find these definitions useful, although playwrights have rarely kept these two modes of drama entirely separate: comic scenes are introduced into a tragedy for 'light relief', as Shakespeare does with the porter in *Macbeth*; and a comedy can darken into something dangerously near tragedy, as *Much Ado about Nothing* does with Claudio's denunciation of Hero at their wedding. Since the end of the 19th century, tragic 'heroes' have no longer had to be kings or leaders, or necessarily male. Most of the plays you read or see during your A2 course might be better described as **tragi-comedies**, and you should be alert to these shifts in tone and how they add to the dramatic effects of a play as a whole.

Developing your definitions of tragedy and comedy

A **tragedy** needs:

- a hero
- a sequence of events leading to the hero's downfall and/or death
- a predominantly serious tone
- a sad ending.

A **comedy** involves:

- stereotypical, stock or representative characters
- a complex plot
- disguise and deception
- mistaken identity

Fig. 6.2 *The Ancient Greek amphitheatre at Epidaurus*

- confusion
- coincidence
- comic routines
- incongruity
- pace (can there be such a thing as a slow comedy?)
- a happy ending.

Comedy covers the full range of humour, from physical slapstick to sophisticated verbal wit. Tragedy is less diverse. Even though its plots may be complex and include many of the dramatic devices listed as comic – disguise, deception, coincidence and confusion, for example – the crucial differences between tragedy and comedy are in situation, **tone** and the motivations of the characters.

Activity

What else can you add to these features of tragedy and comedy, based on your own reading and viewing?

William Shakespeare (1564–1616)

As part of your preparation for the final examination, and to give you a choice of a play by Shakespeare for your A2 coursework, you will need to be familiar with at least one tragedy and one comedy.

Shakespearean tragedy

As we pointed out in Chapter 2, it is difficult to find any of Shakespeare's plays that do not deal with some aspect of love – even the history plays. If you are asked to name a tragedy about love, you will probably say *Romeo and Juliet* or *Othello*. We start here by looking at an extract from the last Act of *Othello*. It comes at the beginning of the final scene of the play. Iago, Othello's supposedly honest and trustworthy lieutenant, has poisoned Othello's mind with suspicions, and destroyed his belief in his wife Desdemona's truthfulness and love. Consumed with jealousy, Othello has made up his mind he must kill her.

Extract A from *Othello*, Act 5 Scene 2

Othello: It is the cause, it is the cause, my soul.
Let me not name it to you, you chaste stars.
It is the cause. Yet I'll not shed her blood,
Nor scar that whiter skin of hers than snow,
And smooth as monumental alabaster.
Yet she must die, else she'll betray more men.
Put out the light, and then put out the light.
If I quench thee, thou flaming minister,
I can again thy former light restore
Should I repent me; but once put out thy light,
Thou cunning'st pattern of excelling nature,
I know not where is that Promethean heat
That can thy light relume. When I have plucked thy rose
I cannot give it vital growth again.
It needs must wither. I'll smell thee on the tree.
(*He kisses her*)
O balmy breath, that dost almost persuade

Fig. 6.3 *Othello agonises by Desdemona's body*

	Justice to break her sword! One more, one more.
	Be thus when thou art dead, and I will kill thee
	And love thee after. One more, and that's the last.
	(*He kisses her*)
	So sweet was ne'er so fatal. I must weep
	But they are cruel tears. This sorrow's heavenly,
	It strikes where it doth love. She wakes.
Desdemona:	Who's there? Othello?
Othello:	Ay, Desdemona.
Desdemona:	Will you come to bed, my lord?
Othello:	Have you prayed tonight, Desdemona?
Desdemona:	Ay, my lord.
Othello:	If you bethink yourself of any crime
	Unreconciled as yet to heaven and grace,
	Solicit for it straight.
Desdemona:	Alack, my lord, what may you mean by that?
Othello:	Well, do it, and be brief. I will walk by.
	I would not kill thy unprep'arèd spirit.
	No, heavens forfend! I would not kill thy soul.
Desdemona:	Talk you of killing?
Othello:	Ay, I do.
Desdemona:	Then heaven have mercy on me.
Othello:	Amen, with all my heart.
Desdemona:	If you say so, I hope you will not kill me.
Othello:	Hum!
Desdemona:	And yet I fear you, for you're fatal then
	When your eyes roll so. Why I should fear I know not,
	Since guiltiness I know not, but yet I feel I fear.
Othello:	Think on thy sins.
Desdemona:	They are loves I bear to you.
Othello:	Ay, and for that thou diest.
Desdemona:	That death's unnatural that kills for loving.
	Alas, why gnaw you so your nether lip?
	Some bloody passion shakes your very frame.

	These are portents, but yet I hope, I hope
	They do not point on me.
Othello:	Peace, and be still.
Desdemona:	I will so. What's the matter?
Othello:	That handkerchief which I so loved and gave thee,
	thou gav'st to Cassio.
Desdemona:	No, by my life and soul. Send for the man
	And ask him.
Othello:	Sweet soul, take heed, take heed of perjury.
	Thou art on thy death bed.
Desdemona:	Ay, but not yet to die.
Othello:	Presently.
	Therefore confess thee freely of thy sin,
	For to deny each article with oath
	Cannot remove nor choke the strong conception
	That I do groan withal. Thou art to die.
Desdemona:	Then Lord have mercy on me.
Othello:	I say amen.
Desdemona:	And have you mercy, too. I never did
	Offend you in my life, never loved Cassio
	But with such general warranty of heaven
	As I might love. I never gave him token.
Othello:	By heaven, I saw my handkerchief in's hand.
	O perjured woman! Thou dost stone my heart,
	And makes me call what I intend to do
	A murder, which I thought a sacrifice.
	I saw the handkerchief.
Desdemona:	He found it, then.
	I never gave it him. Send for him hither.
	Let him confess a truth.
Othello:	He hath confessed.
Desdemona:	What, my lord?
Othello:	That he hath usèd thee.
Desdemona:	How, unlawfully?
Othello:	Ay.
Desdemona:	He will not say so.
Othello:	No, his mouth is stopped.
	Honest Iago hath ta'en order for't.
Desdemona:	O, my fear interprets! What, is he dead?
Othello:	Had all his hairs been lives, my great revenge
	Had stomach for them all.
Desdemona:	Alas, he is betrayed, and I undone.
Othello:	Out, strumpet! Weep'st thou for him to my face?
Desdemona:	O, banish me, my lord, but kill me not.
Othello:	(*attacking her*) Down, strumpet.
Desdemona:	Kill me tomorrow; let me live tonight.
Othello:	Nay, an you strive –
Desdemona:	But half an hour.
Othello:	Being done, there is no pause.
Desdemona:	But while I say one prayer.
Othello:	It is too late. (*He smothers her*)
Desdemona:	O Lord, Lord, Lord!
Emilia:	(*within*) My lord, my lord, what ho, my lord, my lord!
Othello:	What noise is this? Not dead? Not yet quite dead?
	I that am cruel am yet merciful.
	I would not have thee linger in thy pain.
	So, so.

Emilia:	(*within*) What ho, my lord, my lord!
Othello:	Who's there?
Emilia:	(*within*) O, good my lord, I would speak a word with you.
Othello:	Yes. – 'Tis Emilia. – By and by! – She's dead.
	'Tis like she comes to speak of Cassio's death.
	The noise was high. Ha! No more moving.
	Still as the grave. Shall she come in? Were't good?
	I think she stirs again. No. What's best to do?
	If she come in, she'll sure speak to my wife.
	My wife, my wife! What wife? I ha' no wife.
	O insupportable, O heavy hour!
	Methinks it should be now a huge eclipse
	Of sun and moon, and that th' affrighted globe
	Should yawn at alteration.

Act 5 Scene 2 lines 1–109

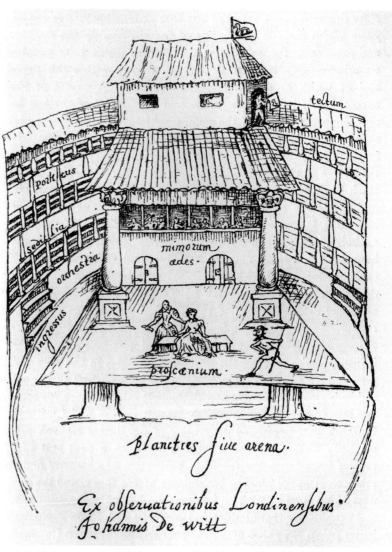

Fig. 6.4 *The apron stage of Shakespeare's Globe Theatre. Sketch by Johannes de Witt*

■ Questions

AO1: Developing an informed response to the text

■ What reasons does Othello give for killing Desdemona?

■ Try to visualise what is happening in this scene. How does Shakespeare create dramatic tension between Othello and Desdemona?

AO2: Understanding how form, structure and language shape meaning

■ How does Othello's language in this scene reflect his state of mind?

■ Analyse the meaning and effect of the images in Othello's first speech in this scene.

■ What do you notice about Shakespeare's use of blank verse in this scene?

AO3: Exploring connections, comparisons and the interpretations of other readers

■ The kiss is a motif in the literature of love in all genres. What do Othello's kisses mean in this extract?

■ Where else in the play does Othello kiss Desdemona? What does he say then, and what do his kisses mean at those moments?

■ Compare Othello's kisses and their significance with kisses in other texts you have read.

■ At the end of Act IV Desdemona sings the 'willow song'. Compare Shakespeare's uses of songs in his tragedies and his comedies.

AO4: Understanding the significance and influence of contexts

■ In what ways does this scene reflect male attitudes to women in the 16th century?

■ Further reading

■ Tragedies and problem plays by Shakespeare: *King Lear, Hamlet, Macbeth, Antony and Cleopatra, The Winter's Tale, Measure for Measure*

Other Jacobean tragedies:

■ *The Duchess of Malfi* by John Webster (1578–1632). The Duchess is a young widow who falls in love with and secretly marries her steward Antonio. Her cruel brothers resent her actions in marrying a man who is socially inferior, and murder her, her husband and her children. Webster's play is more 'gothic' in atmosphere than Shakespeare's tragedies, but it is interesting to compare their treatments of characters and uses of poetic drama.

■ *A Woman Killed with Kindness* by Thomas Heywood (1574–1641). This is an early domestic tragedy set in a middle-class household, and featuring a seducer, a cuckolded husband and an unfaithful wife, punished by being separated permanently from her husband and children. It would be interesting to compare with Shakespeare's and Webster's uses of high-born **protagonists**, and also with more modern realist dramas set in ordinary domestic settings, like *The Doll's House* by Henrik Ibsen (1828–1906), *The Widowing of Mrs Holroyd* by D.H. Lawrence (1885–1930) and *Look Back in Anger* by John Osborne (1929–94).

Other Jacobean tragedies explore the darker sides of love, sex, passion, violence and death. The brief notes of their dominant themes will give you some idea of the flavour of these plays:

■ *The White Devil* (1608–9) by John Webster (adultery, murder and destructive passions)

■ *Women Beware Women* (1614) by Thomas Middleton (seduction, incest, the erotic and destructive power of money)

■ *The Changeling* (1622) by Thomas Middleton (murder, sex and madness)

■ *'Tis Pity She's a Whore* (1632) by John Ford (incestuous love).

Shakespearean comedy

As You Like It is Shakespeare's **pastoral comedy**, set mainly in the fictional but very recognisably rural English landscape of the Forest of Arden. At the beginning of the play, the hero and heroine, Rosalind and Orlando meet at the court of her wicked uncle, and fall in love at first sight, but are quickly separated. Rosalind is banished from court, and flees to the forest, disguised as a boy – Ganymede – accompanied by her cousin, Celia. Orlando is driven from his home by his cruel brother and also ends up in the forest. Just before this extract begins, Celia has been teasing Rosalind about the man who has been carving her name on trees and writing bad poems to her:

Extract B1 from *As You Like It*

Celia:	It is young Orlando, that tripped up the wrestler's heels and your heart, both in an instant.
Rosalind:	Nay, but the devil take mocking; speak sad brow and true maid.
Celia:	I'faith, coz, 'tis he.
Rosalind:	Orlando!
Celia:	Orlando.
Rosalind:	Alas the day, what shall I do with my doublet and hose? What did he when thou sawest him? What said he? How looked he? Wherein went he? What makes he here? Did he ask for me? Where remains he? How parted he with thee? And when shalt thou see him again? Answer me in one word.

Act 3 Scene 2 lines 207–217

Shortly afterwards in the same scene, Orlando and Rosalind meet. He does not recognise her, and in the following extract, Ganymede/Rosalind offers to cure Orlando of his love-sickness by role-playing the woman he loves.

Extract B2 from *As You Like It*

Orlando:	Where dwell you, pretty youth?
Rosalind:	With this shepherdess, my sister, here in the skirts of the forest, like fringe upon a petticoat.
Orlando:	Are you native of this place?
Rosalind:	As the <u>cony</u> that you see dwell where she is <u>kindled</u>.
Orlando:	Your accent is something finer than you could purchase in so removed a dwelling.
Rosalind:	I have been told so of many; but indeed an old religious uncle of mine taught me to speak, who was in his youth an inland man – one that knew courtship too well, for there he fell in love. I have heard him read many lectures against it, and I thank God I am not a woman, to be touched with so many giddy offences as he hath generally taxed their whole sex withal.
Orlando:	Can you remember any of the principal evils that he laid to the charge of women?
Rosalind:	There were none principal, they were all like one another as halfpence are, every one fault seeming monstrous till his fellow-fault came to match it.
Orlando:	I prithee, recount some of them.
Rosalind:	No, I will not cast away my physic but on those that are sick. There is a man haunts the forest that abuses our young plants with carving 'Rosalind' on their barks;

Modern language

cony: rabbit

kindled: born

hangs odes upon hawthorns, and elegies on brambles; all, forsooth, deifying the name of Rosalind. If I could meet that fancy-monger, I would give him some good counsel, for he seems to have the <u>quotidian</u> of love upon him.

Orlando: I am he that is so love-shaked. I pray you, tell me your remedy.

Rosalind: There is none of my uncle's marks upon you. He taught me how to know a man in love; in which cage of rushes I am sure you are not prisoner.

Orlando: What were his marks?

Rosalind: A lean cheek, which you have not; a blue eye and sunken, which you have not; an unquestionable spirit, which you have not; a beard neglected, which you have not – but I pardon you for that, for simply your having in beard is a younger brother's revenue. Then your hose should be ungartered, your bonnet unbanded, your sleeve unbuttoned, your shoe untied, and everything about you demonstrating a careless desolation. But you are no such man: you are rather point-device in your accoutrements, as loving yourself, than seeming the lover of any other.

Orlando: Fair youth, I would I could make thee believe I love.

Rosalind: Me believe it? You may as soon make her that you love believe it, which I warrant she is apter to do than to confess she does: that is one of the points in the which women still give the lie to their consciences. But in good sooth, are you he that hangs the verses on the trees, wherein Rosalind is so admired?

Orlando: I swear to thee, youth, by the white hand of Rosalind, I am that he, that unfortunate he.

Rosalind: But are you so much in love as your rhymes speak?

Orlando: Neither rhyme nor reason can express how much.

Rosalind: Love is merely a madness and, I tell you, deserves as well a dark house and a whip as madmen do; and the reason why they are not so punished and cured is that the lunacy is so ordinary that the whippers are in love too. Yet I profess curing it by counsel.

Orlando: Did you ever cure any so?

Rosalind: Yes, one, and in this manner. He was to imagine me his love, his mistress; and I set him every day to woo me. At which time would I, being but a moonish youth, grieve, be effeminate, changeable, longing and liking, proud, fantastical, apish, shallow, inconstant, full of tears, full of smiles; for every passion something, and for no passion truly anything, as boys and women are for the most part cattle of this colour; would now like him, now loathe him; then entertain him, then forswear him; now weep for him, then spit at him; that I drave my suitor from his mad humour of love to a living humour of madness – which was, to forswear the full stream of the world and to live in a nook merely monastic. And thus I cured him, and this way will I take upon me to wash your liver as clean as a sound sheep's heart, that there shall not be one spot of love in't.

Orlando: I would not be cured, youth.

Rosalind: I would cure you, if you would but call me 'Rosalind', and come every day to my cote, and woo me.

■ Modern language

quotidian: recurring fever

■ Further reading

■ Shakespeare's comedies, *The Taming of the Shrew, A Midsummer Night's Dream, Much Ado about Nothing, Twelfth Night*

■ 16th- and 17th-century love poetry – Shakespeare's *Sonnets*

■ *The Genius of Shakespeare* by Jonathan Bate (Picador)

■ *1599: a Year in the Life of William Shakespeare* by James Shapiro (Faber). Look especially at Chapter 11 'Simple Truth Suppressed', in which he discusses *As You Like It* in some detail. Shapiro is very clear about his interpretation of the play: when you have read the whole play you may not agree with him!

■ *Shakespeare: a Very Short Introduction* by Germaine Greer (Oxford). To clarify your knowledge about the role of women during the period, look at the beginning of Chapter 6, in which Greer explains 16th-century views about betrothals and marriage, and Shakespeare's attitudes to women.

> Orlando: Now, by the faith of my love, I will. Tell me where it is.
> Rosalind: Go with me to it and I'll show it you: and by the way you shall tell me where in the forest you live. Will you go?
> Orlando: With all my heart, good youth.
> Rosalind: Nay, you must call me 'Rosalind'. *Exeunt*

Act 3 Scene 2 lines 323–416

Questions

AO1: Developing an informed response to the text

- What impressions do you have of Rosalind in these two extracts?
- What kinds of love are being presented here?

AO2: Understanding how form, structure and language shape meaning

- How does Shakespeare create comedy in these two scenes?

AO3: Exploring connections, comparisons and the interpretations of other readers

- What scenes from other plays by Shakespeare do these extracts remind you of?

AO4: Understanding the significance and influence of contexts

- How does Shakespeare exploit the fact that in his theatre women's parts were played by boys?
- What use does Shakespeare make here of the conventions found in 16th-century love poetry about the behaviour of men and women in love?

The importance of endings

It has been said that one of the pleasures of comedy is that we know what is going to happen, and enjoy watching events being played out to a happy ending, but in his comedies Shakespeare always casts a little doubt on this 'happiness' which makes it important to pay as much attention to his final scenes as to his opening ones. He certainly does not give us the 'they all lived happily ever after' of the fairy tale, or a romantic novel. In *As You Like It*, as well as Rosalind and Orlando, he gives us three other pairs of lovers, reflecting different kinds of love. They are brought together at the end, but at least one of the three pairs (Touchstone and Audrey) make a long and happy marriage look a very doubtful prospect.

Activity

Think about this aspect of Shakespeare's use of dramatic structure in relation to the endings of other Shakespearean comedies you read or see, and about the ways other playwrights use endings.

Drama in the 17th and 18th centuries: Restoration comedy (or comedy of manners)

During the English Civil War (1642–51) theatres were closed by the Puritans. When the monarchy was restored under Charles II in 1660, playwrights turned from tragedy to comedy, producing plays much more related in tone to the witty poems of the Cavalier poets and Marvell's *Coy Mistress* in their attitudes to love, sex and marriage.

Fig. 6.5 *An example of a 19th century theatre, Drury Lane Theatre in London, complete with proscenium arch, pit and boxes*

The **subject matter** of Restoration comedy is:

▦ the presentation of a superficial, sophisticated, predominantly urban society

▦ fashionable behaviour among the leisured upper classes

▦ departures from normal, civilised behaviour

▦ the absurdities of fashion

▦ social ambition

▦ relations between the sexes

▦ women's roles in society

▦ money and marriage.

The **style** involves:

▦ complex plots that depend on intrigue, double crossing and deception, betrayal and revenge

▦ the use of stock characters – cast lists include:

   – fashionable young men about town; dissolute rakes; jealous husbands; con men; fops

   – beautiful young women; ugly old women

   – gullible people of both sexes

   – loyal and disloyal servants

▦ brittle-mannered language which gives a satirical edge to the presentation of situations, characters and dialogue

▦ plenty of **dramatic irony**

▦ jokes at the expense of country people.

The **themes** are:

- social comment and criticism
- critiques of marriage and relationships between the sexes
- the power of money.

The Way of the World by William Congreve (1670–1729)

The Way of the World is a typical Restoration comedy in plot(s), characters and style. It satirises a group of upper-class Londoners, whose lives are intertwined in a complicated net of previous love affairs, inheritances and scores to settle, especially between the women. The group includes the usual characters:

- two men about town: immoral Mr Fainall and Mirabell, the hero
- three young women:
  - unhappily married Mrs Fainall
  - Mrs Marwood, widow and troublemaker
  - the heroine, Millamant: beautiful, witty, independent-minded
- a dominating but gullible old lady, Lady Wishfort
- a collection of loyal servants who exist to further the plots of their superiors
- an uncle, a nephew and two stupid, foppish hangers-on, for added comic effect.

Fig. 6.6 *Scene from* **The Way of the World**

Extract C1 from *The Way of the World*

At the beginning of the play, Mirabell is discussing his feelings for the heroine, Millamant, with his 'friend', the dissolute rake, Fainall. Remember that in the early 18th century, 'mistress' and 'lover' did not carry the sexual **connotations** they do today.

Fainall: For a passionate lover, methinks you are a man somewhat too discerning in the failings of your mistress.

Mirabell: And for a discerning man, somewhat too passionate a lover; for I like her with all her faults; nay, like her for her faults. Her follies are so natural, or so artful, that they become her; and those affectations which in another woman would be odious, serve but to make her more agreeable. I'll tell thee, Fainall, she once used me with that insolence, that in revenge I took her to pieces; sifted her, and separated her failings; I studied 'em and got 'em by rote. The catalogue was so large that I was not without hopes one day or other to hate her heartily: to which end I so used myself to think of 'em that at length, contrary to my design and expectation, they gave me every hour less and less disturbance; till in a few days it became habitual to me to remember 'em without being displeased. They are now grown as familiar to me as my own frailties; and in all probability, in a little time longer I shall like 'em as well.

Activity

What is your impression of Mirabell here?

We see Mirabell and Millamant alone together in only two scenes. At the end of Act 2 he tries to talk seriously to Millamant, but she refuses to listen to him, showing herself to be as wilful and full of 'infinite variety' as Cleopatra. She says nothing that makes her feelings for him explicit. The actor's body language, inflections, expressions and gestures would have to convey what she really feels about him, and let the audience see the woman that Mirabell describes to Fainall, and the reasons why he has fallen in love with her.

Extract C2 from *The Way of the World*

In this extract, from Act 4, Millamant and Mirabell discuss their terms for a prenuptial contract.

Millamant: (…) Ah! I'll never marry unless I am first made sure of my will and pleasure.

Mirabell: Would you have 'em both before marriage? Or will you be contented with the first now, and stay for the other till after grace?

Millamant: Ah, don't be impertinent! – My dear liberty, shall I leave thee? My faithful solitude, my darling contemplation, must I bid you then adieu? Adieu, my morning thoughts, agreeable wakings, indolent slumbers, all *ye douceurs, ye sommeils du matin*, adieu. – I can't do't, 'tis more than impossible. – Positively Mirabell, I'll lie a-bed in a morning as long as I please.

Mirabell: Then I'll get up in a morning as early as I please.

Millamant: Ah, idle creature, get up when you will – and d'ye hear, I won't be called names after I'm married; positively I won't be called names.

Mirabell: Names!

Millamant: Ay, as wife, spouse, my dear, joy, jewel, love, sweetheart and the rest of that nauseous cant in which men and their wives are so fulsomely familiar; I shall never bear that. – Good Mirabell, don't let us be familiar or fond, nor kiss before folks, like my Lady Fadler and Sir Francis; nor go to Hyde Park together the first Sunday in a new chariot, to provoke eyes and whispers, and then never to be seen there together again, as if we were proud of one another the first week, and ashamed of one another for ever after. Let us never visit together, nor go to a play together, but let us be very strange and well-bred; let us be as strange as if we had been married a great while, and as well bred as if we were not married at all.

Mirabell: Have you any more conditions to offer? Hitherto your demands are pretty reasonable.

Millamant: Trifles. – As liberty to pay and receive visits to and from whom I please; to write and receive letters, without interrogatories or wry faces on your part. To wear what I please, and choose conversation with regard only to my own taste; to have no obligation upon me to converse with wits that I don't like, because they are your acquaintance, or to be intimate with fools, because they may be your relations. Come to dinner when I please; dine in my dressing room when I'm out of humour, without giving a reason. To have my closet inviolate; to be sole empress of my tea-table, which you must never presume to approach without first asking leave. And lastly, wherever I am, you shall always knock at the door before you come in. These articles subscribed, if I continue to endure you a little longer, I may by degrees dwindle into a wife.

Mirabell: Your bill of fare is something advanced in this latter account. Well, have I liberty to offer conditions – that when you are dwindled into a wife, I may not be beyond measure enlarged into a husband?

Millamant: You have free leave; propose your utmost, speak and spare not.

Mirabell: I thank you. *Inprimis* then, I covenant that your acquaintance be general; that you admit no sworn confidante, or intimate of your own sex; no she-friend to screen her affairs under your countenance and tempt you to make trial of a mutual secrecy. No decoy-duck to wheedle you a fop, scrambling to the play in a mask; then bring you home in a pretended fright, when you think you shall be found out – and rail at me for missing the play, and disappointing the frolic, which you had to pick me up and prove my constancy.

Millamant: Detestable *inprimis*! I go to the play in a mask!

Mirabell: *Item*, I article that you continue to like your own face, as long as I shall. And while it passes current with me, that you endeavour not to new coin it. To which end, together with all vizards for the day, I prohibit all masks for the night, made of oiled skins and I know not what – hog's bones, hare's-gall, pig-water, and the marrow of a roasted cat. In short, I forbid all commerce with the gentlewoman in what-d'ye-call-it Court. *Item*, I shut my doors against all bawds with baskets, and penny-worths of muslin, china, fans, atlases etc, etc. *Item*, when you shall be breeding –

Millamant: Ah! Name it not.

Mirabell: Which may be presumed, with a blessing on our endeavours –

Millamant: Odious endeavours!

Mirabell: I denounce against all strait-lacing, squeezing for a shape, till you mould my boy's head like a sugar-loaf; and instead of a man-child, make me the father to a crooked billet. Lastly, to the dominion of the tea-table I submit – but with proviso that you exceed not in your province, but restrain yourself to native and simple tea-table drinks, as tea, chocolate and coffee. As likewise, to genuine and authorised tea-table talk, such as mending of fashions, spoiling reputations, railing at absent friends, and so forth; but that on no account you encroach upon the men's prerogative, and presume to drink healths, or toast fellows; for prevention of which, I banish all foreign forces, all auxiliaries to the tea-table, as orange-brandy, all aniseed, cinnamon, citron and Barbadoes waters, together with ratafia and the most noble spirit of clary. But for cowslip wine, poppy-water and all dormitives, those I allow. – These provisos admitted, in other things I may prove a tractable and complying husband.

Modern language

inprimis: first

atlases: silk/satin fabric from the East

orange-brandy; aniseed, cinnamon, citron and Barbadoes waters; ratafia; clary: all strong alcoholic drinks

Millamant: Oh horrid provisos! Filthy strong waters! I toast fellows, odious men! I hate your odious provisos.
Mirabell: Then we're agreed. Shall I kiss your hand upon the contract? And here comes one to be a witness to the sealing of the deed.
   (Enter Mrs Fainall)
Millamant: Fainall, what shall I do? Shall I have him? I think I must have him.

And, of course, she does! At the end of the play, Mirabell clinches his role as the hero by intervening to ensure that the rewards and punishments which the other characters receive are just and appropriate, and the money at stake ends up in the right hands.

Questions

AO1: Developing an informed response to the text

■ Describe what is happening in this extract, on and below its surface.

■ What are your impressions of Mirabell and Millamant and their relationship?

AO2: Understanding how form, structure and language shape meaning

■ Consider the ways Congreve uses language to conceal and reveal the characters' feelings.

AO3: Exploring connections, comparisons and the interpretations of other readers

'Theatrically effective, pure comedy'

'A skirmish in the battle between the sexes'

'A serious exploration of how to combine, love, independence and marriage'

■ Which of these views best matches your own response to this scene?

AO4: Understanding the significance and influence of contexts

■ How much have you learnt from these extracts about early 18th-century society?

🔍 Drama in the 19th century

Poetry and prose were the dominant genres during the 19th century. Popular theatre persisted in music halls, **melodramas** and adaptations of best-selling novels, but the 19th-century plays that are most frequently performed today, and are seen as important in the development of English drama, are translations of plays by writers from Scandinavia and Russia – Henrik Ibsen (1828–1906) and Anton Chekhov (1860–1904).

Henrik Ibsen, a Norwegian, was the most influential on writers in England and later in America. From 1877 he produced realist dramas, focusing on contemporary political and social issues. He tackled controversial aspects of women's rights, and the personal and social causes and consequences of marriage breakdowns, fraud and inherited sexual disease. His work inevitably provoked strong positive and negative reactions from Victorian critics and audiences.

Ibsen combines realism with symbolism in his critiques of society and of relationships between men and women.

Further reading

The main playwrights of the late 17th century and first half of the 18th century, and their best-known plays, with dates of first performances are:

■ *The Man of Mode* (1676) by Sir George Etherege

■ *The Country Wife* (1675), *The Plain Dealer* (1676) by William Wycherley

■ *The Way of the World* (1700) by William Congreve (his last play)

■ *The Beaux Stratagem* (1707) by George Farquhar.

Wycherley and Farquhar pick up on the satirical and comic strand of the contrasts between sophisticated town dwellers and supposedly stupid country people, seen in comedies by Shakespeare and Ben Jonson (1572–1637).

■ *The Beggar's Opera* (1728) by John Gay turns Restoration comedies upside down. It is a ballad opera which makes maximum use of songs and subverts the whole idea of romantic love, with its cast of lower-class criminal characters, a highwayman 'hero' who nearly ends up on the gallows but is released into the hands of his numerous 'wives'. *The Threepenny Opera* by Bertolt Brecht is a 20th-century version of this play.

■ *She Stoops to Conquer* by Oliver Goldsmith (1730–74): set in a country inn, and involves cases of mistaken identity on a grand scale.

■ *The Rivals* by Richard Brinsley Sheridan (1751–1816): set in fashionable Bath, and satirises romantic love.

Activity

Think of the resonances of phrases like 'a doll's house' as the title for a play about a wife infantilised by her husband in a conventional 19th-century marriage, or 'ghosts' for a play about the dreadful consequences of secrets about the past hidden for too long from the person who most deserves to know them.

Ibsen's dramatic method is not to lecture his audience or bully it into agreement with his point of view. Instead, he shows the situation and the characters' complex and contradictory actions and reactions. He sets up debates between them which involve the audience in questioning, interpreting and judging what they see and coming to their own decisions about the outcomes. Ibsen's aim was to present a 'truthful vision', not moral lessons with simple solutions to complicated problems.

A Doll's House by Henrik Ibsen (1879)

If you studied the Victorian Literature option for AS you may already have studied A Doll's House as part of your coursework. We will now look at three extracts from Act 3 (the final act of the play) in which Ibsen explores different definitions of love.

Extract D1 from A Doll's House

Mrs Linde is a friend of Nora Helmer, the heroine. Recently, in Nora's home, she has met Nils Krogstad, the man she was once in love with. They had been forced to part because of lack of money and her family responsibilities. Krogstad is blackmailing Nora about a loan which she obtained from him illegally, and he has just been sacked from his job at the bank where Helmer is now Manager, despite Nora's attempts to keep him quiet by asking her husband to keep him on.

Krogstad: When I lost you, it was just as if the ground had slipped away from under my feet. Look at me now: a broken man clinging to the wreck of my life.
Mrs Linde: Help might be near. (…) You said you were like a broken man clinging to the wreck of his life.
Krogstad: And I said it with good reason.
Mrs Linde: And I am like a broken woman clinging to the wreck of her life. Nobody to care about, and nobody to care for.
Krogstad: It was your own choice.
Mrs Linde: At the time there was no other choice.
Krogstad: Well, what of it?
Mrs Linde: Nils, what about us two castaways joining forces?
Krogstad: What's that you say?
Mrs Linde: Two of us on one wreck surely stand a better chance than each on his own.
Krogstad: Kristine!
Mrs Linde: Why do you suppose I came to town?
Krogstad: You mean, you thought of me?
Mrs Linde: Without work I couldn't live. All my life I have worked, for as long as I can remember; that has always been my one great joy. But now I'm completely alone in the world, and feeling horribly empty and forlorn. There's no pleasure in working only for yourself. Nils, give me somebody and something to work for.
Krogstad: I don't believe all this. It's only a woman's hysteria, wanting to be all magnanimous and self-sacrificing.
Mrs Linde: Have you ever known me hysterical before?

Krogstad: Would you really do this? Tell me – do you know all about my past?

Mrs Linde: Yes.

Krogstad: And you know what people think about me?

Mrs Linde: Just now you hinted you thought you might have been a different person with me.

Krogstad: I'm convinced I would.

Mrs Linde: Couldn't it still happen?

Krogstad: Kristine! You know what you are saying, don't you? Yes, you do. I can see you do. Have you really the courage?

Mrs Linde: I need someone to mother, and your children need a mother. We two need each other. Nils, I have faith in what, deep down, you are. With you I can face anything.

Krogstad: Thank you, thank you, Kristine …

Mrs Linde and Krogstad then discuss Nora's situation, and the letter that he has just left revealing her crime to Helmer. Krogstad is now willing to retrieve the letter, but Mrs Linde is convinced that the truth must be known, and Nora's marriage can no longer rest on lies.

Extract D2 from *A Doll's House*

A little later Helmer and Nora return home from a neighbour's party. Nora is acutely aware that Krogstad's letter is waiting to be opened.

Helmer: … Ah, it's wonderful to be back in our own home again, and quite alone with you. How irresistibly lovely you are, Nora!

Nora: Don't look at me like that, Torvald!

Helmer: Can't I look at my most treasured possession? At all this loveliness that is mine, and mine alone, completely and utterly mine.

Nora: (*walks round to the other side of the table*) You mustn't talk to me like that tonight.

Helmer: (*following her*) You still have the tarantella in your blood, I see. And that makes you even more desirable. Listen! The guests are beginning to leave now …

　　　　(*Softly*) Nora … soon the whole house will be silent.

Nora: I should hope so.

Fig. 6.7 *Torvald and Nora in* **A Doll's House**

Helmer: Of course you do, don't you, Nora my darling? You know, whenever I'm at a party with you … do you know why I never talk to you very much, why I always stand away from you and only steal a quick glance at you now and then … do you know why I do that? It's because I am pretending we are secretly in love, secretly engaged and nobody suspects there is anything between us.

Nora: Yes, yes. I know your thoughts are always with me, of course.

Helmer: And when it's time to go, and I lay your shawl round those shapely, young shoulders, round the exquisite curve of your neck … I pretend that you are my young bride, that we are just leaving our wedding, that I am taking you to our new home for the first time … to be alone with you for the first time … quite alone with your young and trembling loveliness! All evening I've been longing for you, and nothing else. And as I watched you darting and swaying in the tarantella, my blood was on fire … I couldn't bear it any longer … and that's why I brought you down here with me so early.

Nora: Go away, Torvald! Please leave me alone. I won't have it.

Helmer: What's this? It's just your little game isn't it, my little Nora. Won't! Won't! Am I not your husband …?

(There is a knock on the front door)

Interrupted by a visitor, Nora makes up her mind to tell him the truth, and when the visitor leaves, she urges Helmer to read his letters. His reaction to Krogstad's letter is violent – he rejects Nora, calls her 'a hypocrite, a liar and a criminal' whom he will not trust to bring up their children. He is interrupted by a second note from Krogstad, enclosing Nora's IOU with her forged signature on it. Helmer's reaction is 'I am saved! I am saved.' He immediately returns to patronising Nora, who is determined that her marriage is over and she must leave her husband and her children. Before she goes, she insists on having a serious conversation with Helmer – the first she says they have had in eight years of marriage:

Extract D3 from *A Doll's House*

Helmer: You are ill, Nora. You are delirious. I'm half inclined to think you are out of your mind.

Nora: Never have I felt so calm and collected as I do tonight.

Helmer: Calm and collected enough to leave your husband and children?

Nora: Yes.

Helmer: Then only one explanation is possible.

Nora: And that is?

Helmer: You don't love me any more.

Nora: Exactly.

Helmer: Nora! Can you say that?

Nora: I'm desperately sorry, Torvald. Because you have always been so kind to me. But I can't help it. I don't love you any more.

Helmer: *(struggling to keep his composure)* Is that also a 'calm and collected' decision you've made?

Nora: Yes, absolutely calm and collected. That's why I don't want to stay here.

Helmer: And can you account for how I forfeited your love?

Nora: Yes, very easily. It was tonight, when the miracle didn't happen. It was then I realised you weren't the man I thought you were.

Helmer: Explain yourself more clearly. I don't understand.

Nora: For eight years I have been patiently waiting. Because, heavens, I knew miracles didn't happen every day. Then this devastating business started, and I became absolutely convinced that the miracle would happen. All the time Krogstad's letter lay there, it never so much as crossed my mind that you *would* ever submit to that man's conditions. I was absolutely convinced that you would say to him: Tell the whole world if you like. And when that was done …

Helmer: Yes, then what? After I had exposed my own wife to dishonour and shame …

Nora: When that was done, I was absolutely convinced you would come forward and take everything on yourself, and say: I am the guilty one.

Helmer: Nora!

Nora: You mean I'd never let you make such a sacrifice for my sake? Of course not. But what would my story have counted for against yours? – That was the miracle I went in hope and dread of. It was to prevent it that I was ready to end my life.

Helmer: I would gladly toil day and night for you, Nora, enduring all manner of sorrow and distress. But nobody sacrifices his honour for the one he loves.

Nora: Hundreds and thousands of women have.

Helmer: Oh, you think and talk like a stupid child.

Nora: All right. But you neither think nor talk like the man I would want to share my life with.

Questions

AO1: Developing an informed response to the text

- What is going on in these extracts? Explore the text and subtext of the dialogues as fully as you can.

AO2: Understanding how form, structure and language shape meaning

- Consider the ways Ibsen uses language to reveal character in these scenes.
- What different definitions of love is Ibsen working with here?
- Compare the situations of Nora and Mrs Mallard in 'The Story of an Hour' (see p72).
- How do you respond to the ways Ibsen and Chopin use the endings of their stories?

AO3: Exploring connections, comparisons and the interpretations of other readers

- Compare the scenes between Nora and Helmer with the one between Millamant and Mirabell (see pp95–7).
- George Bernard Shaw (1856–1950) was a great admirer of Ibsen's work, and his method of presenting us with questions rather than answers. In *The Quintessence of Ibsenism*, he warns against being too assertive about Ibsen's characters or their motives:

'When you have called Nora a fearless and noble hearted woman or a shocking little liar and an unnatural mother, Helmer a selfish hound or a model father or husband and father, according to your bias, you have said something which is at once true and false, and in both cases perfectly idle.'

- What point about Ibsen's presentation of character is Shaw making here?
- How many similar statements can you make about Nora, Helmer, Mrs Linde and Krogstad?

AO4: Understanding the significance and influence of contexts

- What does this play contribute to your awareness of the position of women in the late 19th century?

Further reading

- Plays by Ibsen:
  - *Ghosts* (1881) – a mother has sheltered her son for too long from the facts of his dissolute father's past.
  - *Hedda Gabler* (1890) – a psychological study of a frustrated heroine, married to the wrong man.
  - *An Enemy of the People* (1882) – public scandal is hushed up to preserve reputations.
- Plays by Chekhov:
  - *Uncle Vanya* (1898)
  - *The Three Sisters* (1900)
  - *The Cherry Orchard* (1904)
  - *The Seagull* (1896).

Nearly every character in *The Seagull* is in love – most of them are unhappy, because their love is not requited, or is rejected, or given to the wrong person.

Chekhov's plays, which he called 'comedies', are more subdued than Ibsen's, always set in provincial Russia where his characters live out boring, or disappointed, lives. There are moments of humour, but the dominant tone is of resignation to the realities of life.

- Plays by Oscar Wilde (1854–1900):
  - *Lady Windermere's Fan* (1892)
  - *A Woman of No Importance* (1893)
  - *The Importance of Being Earnest* (1895).

Wilde continues the 18th-century tradition of combining witty comedy with comment on issues in fashionable contemporary society.

🔍 The 20th century

Bertolt Brecht (1898–1956) had great influence on the development of drama in England, theoretically and practically. He was forced to leave Germany when Hitler came to power in 1933, and spent most of World War Two in exile. On his return to Germany he set up his theatre company, the Berliner Ensemble, and in his work as a dramatist and a director he developed his theories of **epic theatre**. Unlike Ibsen, who used realism to draw his audience's attention to contemporary social issues, Brecht's aim was to create a distance between the audience and the performance – the **alienation effect**. His subject matter was political, and he did not want the audience simply to sympathise or identify with the characters they see on the stage. He wanted people to think about the conditions in society, their own actions and their power, or lack of it, to bring about change. This approach is very different from Ibsen's realism in the ways Brecht tells a story, presents characters, expresses ideas, and stages the action of the play.

The Caucasian Chalk Circle by Bertolt Brecht

The non-realistic staging of this play with its many different locations, and the epic sweep of its narrative, are part of Brecht's alienation technique. Brecht suggested the use of projections, not naturalistic scenery, and the many supporting parts played by a small group of actors. Brecht keeps The Singer and the musicians on stage throughout, and uses songs partly to move the narrative from scene to scene and place to place, and partly to emphasise and comment on the themes of the play, which are human ones of survival and love.

Grusha, the peasant 'heroine', is easy to admire, for her strong will, practicality and outspokenness; the play insists that she is a good person. Early on, when Grusha is trying to escape from the chaos after the Governor's palace has been attacked and the Governor's wife has fled, abandoning her baby son, The Singer comments: 'Terrible is the temptation to do good' as Grusha tries to decide what to do. He sings:

> For a long time she sat with the child.
> Evening came, night came, dawn came.
> Too long she sat, too long she watched
> The soft breathing, the little fists
> Till towards morning the temptation grew too strong.
> She rose, she leaned over, she sighed, she lifted the child
> She carried it off.

This is the start of the episodic narrative of what happens to Grusha and the baby, Michael, how she looks after him through their difficult journeys, and the sacrifices she makes for him, including having to break her promise to wait for the soldier she loves. At the end of the play, the Governor's wife reappears to claim her child, who has inherited all his father's wealth. A trial to determine whether she or Grusha is Michael's true mother is conducted by Azdak, an ex petty criminal who has been democratically elected Judge by the community.

Extract E from *The Caucasian Chalk Circle*, Scene 6

Azdak: *(beckons Grusha towards him and bends not unkindly towards her.)* I've noticed that you have a soft spot for justice. I don't believe he's your child, but if he were yours, woman, wouldn't you want him to be rich? You'd only have to say he isn't yours and at once he'd have a palace, scores of horses in this stable, scores of beggars on his doorstep, scores of soldiers in his service, and scores of petitioners in his courtyard. Now, what d'you say? Don't you want him to be rich?

(Grusha is silent)

The Singer: Listen now to what the angry girl thought, but didn't say. *(He sings)*

> He who wears shoes of gold
> Tramples on the weak and old
> Does evil all day long
> And mocks at wrong.

Azdak: I think I understand you, woman.

Grusha: I won't give him away. I've brought him up, and he knows me.

(Enter Shauva, the judge's assistant, with the child)

The Governor's Wife: It's in rags!

Grusha: That's not true. I wasn't given time to put on his good shirt.

The Governor's Wife: It's been in a pig-sty.

Grusha: *(furious)* I'm no pig, but there are others who are. Where did you leave your child?

The Governor's Wife: I'll let you have it, you vulgar person. *(She is about to throw herself on Grusha, but is restrained by her lawyers.)* She's a criminal! She must be flogged! Right away!

The Second Lawyer: *(holding his hand over her mouth)* Most gracious Natella Abashvili, you promised …Your Worship, the plaintiff's nerves …

Azdak: Plaintiff and defendant! The Court has listened to your case, and has come to no decision as to who the real mother of this child is. I as judge have the duty of choosing a mother for the child. I'll make a test. Shauva, get a piece of chalk and draw a circle on the floor. *(Shauva does so.)* Now place the child in the centre. *(Shauva puts Michael, who smiles at Grusha, in the centre of the circle.)*

Plaintiff and defendant, stand near the circle, both of you.

(The Governor's Wife and Grusha step up to the circle)

Now each of you take the child by a hand. The true mother is she who has the strength to pull the child out of the circle towards herself.

The Second Lawyer: *(quickly)* High Court of Justice, I protest! I object that the fate of the great Abashvili estates, which are bound up with the child as the heir, should be made dependent on such a doubtful wrestling match. Moreover, my client does not command the same physical strength as this person, who is accustomed to physical work.

Azdak: She looks pretty well fed to me. Pull!

(The Governor's Wife pulls the child out of the circle to her side. Grusha has let it go and stands aghast.)

The First Lawyer: *(congratulating the Governor's Wife)* What did I say! The bonds of blood!

Azdak: (*to Grusha*) What's the matter with you? You didn't pull!

Grusha: I didn't hold on to him. (*She runs to Azdak*) Your Worship, I take back everything I said against you. I ask your forgiveness. If I could just keep him until he can speak properly. He knows only a few words.

Azdak: Don't influence the Court! I bet you know only twenty yourself. All right, I'll do the test once more, to make certain.

(*The two women take up positions again.*)

Azdak: Pull!

(*Again Grusha lets go of the child.*)

Grusha: (*in despair*) I've brought him up! Am I to tear him to pieces? I can't do it!

Azdak: (*rising*) And in this manner the Court has established the true mother.

(*To Grusha*) Take your child and be off with it. I advise you not to stay in town with him.

(*To the Governor's Wife*) And you disappear before I fine you for fraud. Your estates fall to the city. A playground for children will be made out of them. They need one, and I have decided it shall be called after me – The Garden of Azdak.

And like a Shakespearean or Restoration comedy, the play ends with Grusha reunited with the man she has always loved, and a dance.

■ Questions

AO1: Developing an informed response to the text

■ What impressions do you have of Grusha and the Governor's wife in this scene?

■ What is your opinion of Azdak as judge?

■ What definitions of love is the play offering to the audience?

AO2: Understanding how form, structure and language shape meaning

■ This scene is the climax of the play. How does Brecht make it dramatic?

AO3: Exploring connections, comparisons and the interpretations of other readers

■ Compare this play with any other 20th-century plays you think reflect some of Brecht's theatrical ideas and influence:

– use of projections, video and song to counterpoint or highlight the significance of the action on stage

– non-realistic settings

– episodic structure

– flexible movement between 'scenes'

– political message.

■ Compare Grusha with other heroines in plays you have read about love.

AO4: Understanding the significance and influence of contexts

Brecht bases Azdak's judgement on the story of the Judgement of Solomon in the Bible (1 Kings Chapter 16 verses 16–27).

■ Do you think Brecht's play reflects a 20th-century political context, or do you consider his message in it to be universal?

🔍 The second half of the 20th century

The nearer you get to the 21st century in your wider reading of the literature of love, the more you will have to turn to musicals, films and TV soaps to find texts that focus on romantic love. In 1968 the removal of the Lord Chamberlain's responsibility for censoring plays made it possible to write about sexual relationships, which could not be explicitly dealt with previously. Plays like Mark Ravenhill's *Shopping and F***ing* (1996) treat sex as a matter of economics, and love as a commodity – rather like some 17th- and 18th-century comedies. When love is the subject of modern drama, the 20th-century preoccupation with problems and difficulties in human relationships tends to dominate, although some playwrights take a less bleak view of love in the late 20th century.

Translations by Brian Friel (1929–)

Brian Friel was born in Derry, on the borders of Northern Ireland and Eire. His plays are rooted in the long history of conflict between Ireland and England, hostility within Ireland itself, and the problems of communities divided by religion and language.

Translations was first performed in 1981. The play is set in rural Donegal, and his subject is the colonisation of Ireland by the English. The play is set in the 1830s, a dramatic device to distance the audience from its contemporary context of the situation in Northern Ireland in the 1980s. Friel has chosen a traditional dramatic form for his play – the action covers less than a week, and is divided into three Acts; the setting is realistic – the classroom of an Irish hedge school, where some country people come to learn the basics of reading, writing and mathematics, and others come to learn to speak and read Latin and Greek from the master and his son.

Friel's theme is a political one: how people are divided by language, and how a way of life can be doomed by domination by a foreign power that imposes itself on the native people. We soon learn that the hedge school is threatened by the new national school in the area, where education in English will be compulsory. At the same time, a survey of the area is being carried out by the English Royal Engineers, to map the countryside and translate the Irish place names into English.

Translations is a typical later 20th-century play in its treatment of serious social and political issues, and a play in which love is a significant strand, but not the primary focus of the drama. Friel's great skill as a dramatist is to create a play in which, although the script is written in English, the audience quickly understands that the local people are speaking in Irish, and that the English and the Irish can't understand each other without the help of an interpreter. This has some comic results at first, but in the extract that follows it creates a scene of great tenderness between the English lieutenant, George Yolland, and the Irish girl Maire Chatach. Yolland is new to Ireland, and his view of the place is a romanticised one, but he appreciates its beauty and its culture and has begun to try to learn some of the language, through the place names that his job forces him to anglicise. Earlier in the play we see he is aware of the damaging consequences of his job, when he calls it 'an eviction of sorts … something is being eroded'.

In this extract Yolland and Maire have just come away from a village dance, and are alone together. At first they use their own separate languages, then Yolland tries very simple English and then Maire tries Latin, both with equally frustrating results. Eventually, Yolland finds a way of communicating with her.

Extract F from *Translations*, Act 3 Scene 2

(Yolland extends his hand to Maire. She turns away from him and moves slowly across the stage.)

Yolland: Maire.

(She still moves away.)

Maire Chatach.

(She still moves away.)

Bun na hAbhann?

(He says the name very softly, almost privately, very tentatively, as if he were searching for a sound she might respond to. He tries again.)

Druim Dubh?

(Maire stops. She is listening. Yolland is encouraged.)

Poll na gCaorach. Lis Maol.

(Maire turns towards him.)

Lis na nGall.

Maire: Lis na nGradh.

(They are now facing each other and begin moving – almost imperceptibly – towards one another.)

Carraig an Phoill.

Yolland: Carraig na Ri. Loch na nEan.

Maire: Loch an Iubhair. Machaire Buidhe.

Yolland: Machaire Mor. Cnoc na Mona.

Maire: Cnoc na nGabhar.

Yolland: Mullach.

Maire: Port.

Yolland: Tor.

Maire: Lag.

(She holds out her hands to Yolland. Each now speaks almost to himself/herself.)

Yolland: I wish to God you could understand me.

Maire: Soft hands; a gentleman's hands.

Yolland: Because if you could understand me I could tell you how I spend my days either thinking of you or gazing up at your house in the hope that you'll appear even for a second.

Maire: Every evening you walk by yourself along the Tra Bhan and every morning you wash yourself in front of your tent.

Yolland: I would tell you how beautiful you are, curly-headed Maire. I would so like to tell you how beautiful you are.

Maire: Your arms are long and thin and the skin on your shoulders is very white.

Yolland: I would tell you …

Maire: Don't stop – I know what you're saying.

Yolland: I would tell you how I want to be here – to live here – always– with you – always, always.

Maire: 'Always'? What is that word – 'always'?

Yolland: Yes- yes; always.

Maire: You're trembling.

Yolland: Yes, I'm trembling because of you.

Maire: I'm trembling too. *(She holds his face in her hand.)*

Yolland: I've made up my mind …

Maire: Shhhh.

Yolland: I'm not going to leave here …

Maire: Shhh – listen to me. I want you, too, soldier.

Yolland: Don't stop – I know what you're saying.

Maire: I want to live with you – anywhere – anywhere at all – always – always.

Further reading

Irish drama

- *Playboy of the Western World* by J. M. Synge (1907)
- *Juno and the Paycock* (1923), *The Plough and the Stars* (1924), *Shadow of a Gunman* (1926) by Sean O'Casey
- *The Beauty Queen of Lenhane* by Martin McDonagh (1996)

Yolland: 'Always'? What is that word – 'always'?
Maire: Take me away with you, George.
    (*Pause.*
    Suddenly they kiss.
    Sarah enters. She sees them. She stands shocked, staring at them
(…) *She runs off*).

■ Questions

AO1: Developing an informed response to the text

■ How do you respond to Yolland and Maire in this scene?

AO2: Understanding how form, structure and language shape meaning

■ Look at the way Friel handles the dialogue here. How does he maintain the audience's awareness that the characters are speaking in different languages and at the same time show us that they are communicating with each other?

■ Unlike most of the plays you have read or seen, *Translations* stops at the end of Act 3, rather than being brought to a conclusion.

■ What do you think happens in Act 3? OR (if you have read the whole play), how do you interpret the end of the play?

AO3: Exploring connections, comparisons and the interpretations of other readers

■ Compare this extract with any other scene in drama or prose in which the lovers have difficulty communicating with each other.

AO4: Understanding the significance and influence of contexts

■ Do you think setting the play in the 1830s adds to Friel's political message, or weakens it?

■ If you have read the whole play, would you call it a political play, a tragedy or a love story?

■ Placing the play in its literary context, what do you think is modern about *Translations* and what is traditional?

Betrayal by Harold Pinter (1930–)

Pinter trained as an actor. As well as writing many plays, he has also produced film scripts and adaptations of novels. In 2001 he was awarded the Nobel Prize for Literature. His main concerns in his plays are the power relations between people, and contemporary politics. The speech of his characters is completely **naturalistic**: tentative, repetitive, full of gaps and hesitations. Long pauses, resonant with meaning, are a feature of his style, and what is *not* said forms a powerful undercurrent in his dialogues. His plays tend to baffle people initially, and are open to many different interpretations.

Betrayal was written in 1978. It has only three characters: Emma, Jerry and Robert. The play starts in Spring 1977 and works its way backwards chronologically to end in Winter 1968. The final scene is not just a flashback; it concludes Pinter's slow probing of the development of an affair, enacted in reverse. To appreciate the elegance of the play's structure, and Pinter's skill as a dramatist, you really need to read the whole play. Only then will you fully understand the references and allusions, the subtext, in the dialogue between Emma and Jerry in Scene 1. This extract begins the play.

Extract G from *Betrayal*, Scene 1

Pub. 1977. Spring.

Noon.
Emma is sitting at a corner table. Jerry approaches with drinks,
a pint of bitter for him, a glass of wine for her.
He sits. They smile, toast each other silently, drink.
He sits back and looks at her.
***Jerry**:* Well …
***Emma**:* How are you?
***Jerry**:* All right.
***Emma**:* You look well.
***Jerry**:* Well, I'm not all that well, really.
***Emma**:* Why? What's the matter?
***Jerry**:* Hangover. *(He raises his glass)*
  Cheers. *(He drinks)*
  How are you?
***Emma**:* I'm fine. *(She looks round the bar, back at him.)*
  Just like old times.
***Jerry**:* Mmn. It's been a long time.
***Emma**:* Yes.
  (Pause)
  I thought of you the other day.
***Jerry**:* Good God. Why?
  (She laughs)
  Why?
***Emma**:* Well, it's nice, sometimes, to think back. Isn't it?
***Jerry**:* Absolutely.
  (Pause)
  How's everything?
***Emma**:* Oh, not too bad.
  (Pause)
  Do you know how long it is since we met?
***Jerry**:* Well I came to that private view, when was it –?
***Emma**:* No, I don't mean that.
***Jerry**:* Oh you mean alone?
***Emma**:* Yes.
***Jerry**:* Uuh …
***Emma**:* Two years.
***Jerry**:* Yes, I thought it must be. Mmnn.
  (Pause)
***Emma**:* Long time.
***Jerry**:* Yes. It is.
  (Pause)
  How's it going? The Gallery?
***Emma**:* How do you think it's going?
***Jerry**:* Well. Very well, I would say.
***Emma**:* I'm glad you think so. Well, it is actually. I enjoy it.
***Jerry**:* Funny lot, painters, aren't they?
***Emma**:* They're not at all funny.
***Jerry**:* Aren't they? What a pity.
  (Pause)
  How's Robert?
***Emma**:* When did you last see him?
***Jerry**:* I haven't seen him for months. Don't know why. Why?
***Emma**:* Why what?
***Jerry**:* Why did you ask when I last saw him?

Emma: I just wondered. How's Sam?

Jerry: You mean Judith.

Emma: Do I?

Jerry: You remember the form. I ask about your husband, you ask about my wife.

Emma: Yes, of course. How is your wife?

Questions

AO1: Developing an informed response to the text

■ Playwrights usually use a first scene for exposition – setting the scene, establishing the situation etc. Does that seem to you to be what Pinter is doing in this scene?

■ What is the relationship between Emma and Jerry? How much do you know about both of them by the end of the extract?

AO2: Understanding how form, structure and language shape meaning

■ The theatre critic, Michael Billington, has said 'Language in Pinter's plays operates on many levels … but it is always used with distilled accuracy to reveal character.' How does Pinter present the characters of Emma and Jerry through their language?

■ Some critics have dismissed Pinter's narrative structure in this play as 'conspicuous artifice'. What is your response to the way he handles time, and the way that affects the meaning and impact of the play?

AO3: Exploring connections, comparisons and the interpretations of other readers

■ Pinter could have called his play *Infidelity*. Why do you think he called it *Betrayal*?

AO4: Understanding the significance and influence of contexts

■ *Betrayal* has been called 'a poisoned comedy of manners'. Do you find this an appropriate description?

■ In what ways does it reflect 20th-century attitudes to love and relationships?

Further reading

■ *The Homecoming* (1964) and *Mountain Language* (1988) by Harold Pinter

■ *State of the Nation: British theatre since 1945* by Michael Billington (Faber 2007)

Bent by Martin Sherman (1938–)

Martin Sherman is an American playwright who was involved in the Gay Liberation movement of the 1970s. His play is set in 1930s Germany; the subject is the Nazi persecution of homosexuals. Sherman also reflects the play's time of composition by focusing on the personal and political choices which people have to make when sexual identity and human emotions are at stake. The play received its world premiere in London in 1979.

Act 1 of *Bent* is set in Berlin and Act 2 in the Dachau concentration camp. There the main character, Max, a selfish manipulator of other people, meets Horst, who has been arrested for signing a petition 'to make queers legal'. Max refuses to acknowledge his own homosexuality, choosing instead to be arrested and interned as a Jew. Gradually, as they are forced to carry out mindless and exhausting physical labour under the constant threat of being either shot by the guards, or electrocuted by the prison fence if they try to escape, a relationship develops between them. Initially Max does not accept Horst's love, but at the end of the play, when Horst is shot by a German guard and Max is ordered to dispose of his body, he comes to terms with his own identity and emotions in this dramatic conclusion.

Extract H from *Bent*

(Max walks to Horst's body. He tries to lift it. It is heavy. He manages to pull the body partly up, Horst's head resting against Max's chest. He looks away. He takes Horst, feet dragging on the ground, towards the pit.)

(…)

It's OK. I won't drop you. I'll hold you. If I stand to attention, I can hold you. They'll let me hold you. I won't let you down.

(Silence.)

I never held you before.

(Silence.)

You're safe. I won't drop you.

(Silence.)

Don't worry about the rocks. I'll do yours too. I'll move twice as many each day. I'll do yours too. You don't have to worry about them.

(Silence.)

I won't drop you.

(Silence.)

You know what?

(Silence.)

Horst?

(Silence.)

You know what?

(Silence.)

I think …

(Silence.)

I think I love you.

(Silence.)

Shh! Don't tell anyone. Don't worry about the rocks. I won't drop you. I promise … I think I loved … I can't remember his name. A dancer. I think I loved him too. Don't be jealous. Will I forget your name? No-one else will touch the rocks. I think I loved … some boy, a long time ago. In my father's factory. Hans. That was his name. But the dancer. I don't remember. Don't be jealous. I won't let you drop.

(Silence.)

If I walk a little faster, I can do twice as many rocks a day. I won't let you down.

(Silence.)

I won't let you drop.

(Silence.)

I love you.

(Silence.)

What's wrong with that?

(Silence.)

I won't let you drop. I won't let you drop.

(Silence.)

You know what I did? I got your medicine.

(Silence.)

Hey –

(Silence.)

I don't remember your name.

(Silence.)

Oh my God! This can't be happening.

(*He starts to cry … He drags Horst's body to the pit. He throws it in the pit. He turns and looks at the rocks. He takes a deep breath. He walks over to the rocks and picks one up. He moves it across to the other side. He takes another deep breath. He stands still.*)

One. Two. Three. Four. Five. (*He takes another deep breath.*) Six. Seven. Eight. Nine. Ten.

(*He picks up a rock. He moves it across to the other side.*)
(*He moves another rock.*)
(*He moves another rock.*)
(*He moves another rock.*)
(*He pauses. He takes a deep breath.*)
(*He moves another rock.*)
(*He moves another rock.*)
(*He stops. He tries to take another deep breath. He can't. His hand is trembling. He steadies his hand. He picks up another rock and starts to move it.*)
(*He stops. He drops the rock. He moves towards the pit.*)
(*He jumps into the pit.*)
(*He disappears.*)
(*A long pause.*)
(*He climbs out of the pit.*)
(*He holds Horst's jacket, with the pink triangle on it. He takes off his own jacket. He puts Horst's jacket on.*)
(*He turns and looks at the fence.*)
(*He walks into the fence.*)
(*The fence lights up. It grows brighter and brighter, until the light consumes the stage.*)
(*And blinds the audience.*)
THE END

The play has always been a controversial one, and you will have to decide for yourself whether you think that Max's final words and actions exploit 20th-century knowledge of the Holocaust inappropriately, or movingly transcend any clichéd ideas about sex and romance in its definition of what it means to love another human being.

Checklist for your study of drama texts

Use the prompts below to focus and record your wider reading of drama in preparation for the examination.

The cast list

How much information does it contain about the play?

Stage directions

Are they minimal? (Pinter)
Narrative/descriptive? (Friel, George Bernard Shaw)
Basic information

Setting(s)

A single setting or multiple locations?
Realistic or not?

Props

Realistic or not?

Further reading

20th-century American drama:

- *A View from the Bridge* by Arthur Miller
- *A Streetcar Named Desire* and *Cat on a Hot Tin Roof* by Tennessee Williams
- *Who's Afraid of Virginia Woolf?* by Edward Albee
- *Oleanna* by David Mamet
- *Angels in America* by Tony Kushner.

Structure

- Acts and scenes – how many?
- Links/juxtapositions/movements between scenes?
- Position in the play of climax(es) / turning points / key scenes
- Beginning (exposition) and ending (dénouement)
- Handling of time within the play
- Handling of place

Language

- Features of dialogue(s)
- Use of monologue
- Soliloquy
- Prose
- Verse

The time the play was written, the time it is set in and the time of its first performance

- Are these significant in relation to interpretations of the play?

Does the play explore ideas important at the time it was written?

- Political
- Cultural
- Social
- Intellectual: philosophical, scientific …

How open does the play seem to be to different approaches:

- by different directors and actors
- to staging, setting, costumes
- in performances and interpretations of characters?

In what ways does this play link with other plays you have seen or read?

💡 *Summary*

This chapter has offered you an overview of some of the traditions and influences behind plays being written and produced in England today.

We have focused on:

- some major dramatists, and their approaches to the theme of love
- links between plays and texts in other genres from different periods
- the skills of close reading, analysis and interpretation needed when studying drama texts.

7 Conclusion – a specimen paper

Introduction

All the study and recording you have been doing in the course of working through this book has been leading you to this chapter, which includes a specimen examination paper.

You will need to start thinking about how you are going to:

- use the knowledge you have of the literature of love in the examination
- demonstrate the skills you have been practising through the activities.

Key resources

Before you attempt the specimen paper, we need to review the key tools this book has given you. You should remind yourself of and reread:

1 the guidance in Chapter 1 which consists of questions for use when you are reading a text closely (see pp5–6)

2 the guidance in Chapter 3 both on the ways to prepare for the two examination questions and on the ways you will be assessed

3 the guidance on the definition of a novel, including the features of post-modern novels in Chapter 5

4 the guidance on how to study a drama text in Chapter 6

5 the literary timeline in the grid on pp124–5

6 the reading log you have assembled over the course and while studying Chapters 4, 5 and 6.

Your reading log, whether electronic or in a paper file, is your **key revision tool**. You will have assembled an enormous amount of information about the literature of love and will have organised it by time, genre and gender. All this reading is relevant to the questions on the paper which invite you to read and study the unprepared extracts **closely** as well as to apply your **wider reading** in the literature of love.

The specimen paper

The best way to prepare for the real examination is to **practise answering questions** of the type that will appear on the paper. You can, of course, **make up your own questions** – alone, or in a group, and with the help of your teachers. What follows now is a complete specimen paper. How you use it will be for you to decide. You may wish to use it as a 'mock examination', sitting down and writing for two and a half hours under examination conditions. Or you may wish to look at the questions alone or in a group, brainstorming what materials you might use, how you might structure your answers and then comparing notes, before you write the relevant essays.

Here is the sample examination paper: you should allow yourself two and a half hours to answer it.

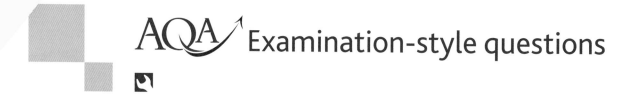

Answer **both** questions.

1   Read the two poems (Extracts A and B) carefully. They were written at different times by different writers.

     Basing your answer on the poems and, where appropriate, your wider reading in the poetry of love, compare the ways the two poets have used poetic form, structure and language to express their thoughts and ideas.   *(40 marks)*

2   Write a comparison of the ways Shakespeare and Hardy present the partings of people who love each other. You should consider:

- the ways the writers' choices of form, structure and language shape your responses to these extracts

- how your wider reading in the literature of love has contributed to your understanding and interpretation of the extracts.   *(40 marks)*

END OF QUESTIONS

Extract A

The poet Michael Drayton (1563–1631) became a page to Sir Henry Goodeere of Polesworth who ensured that he was educated. Drayton fell in love with Sir Henry's daughter who provided the inspiration for *Idea*, a sonnet sequence written in 1619. The following poem is taken from that sequence.

Idea in Sixtie Three Sonnets [61]

Since ther's no helpe, Come let us kisse and part,
Nay, I have done: You get no more of Me,
And I am glad, yea glad with all my heart,
That thus so cleanly I my Selfe can free:
Shake hands for ever, Cancell all our Vowes,
And when We meet at any time againe,
Be it not seene in either of our Browes,
That We one jot of former Love reteyne:
Now at the last gaspe of Love's latest Breath,
When his Pulse fayling, Passion speechlesse lies,
When Faith is kneeling by his bed of Death,
And Innocence is closing up his eyes,
Now if thou would'st, when all have given him over,
From Death to Life thou might'st him yet recover.

Michael Drayton

Extract B

Edna St Vincent Millay (1892–1950) was an American lyrical poet and the first woman to receive the Pulitzer Prize for poetry. She was also known for her unconventional bohemian lifestyle and for her many love affairs with both men and women. She had a significant relationship with the poet George Dillon, for whom this and many other sonnets were written.

If I should learn, in some quite casual way

If I should learn, in some quite casual way,
That you were gone, not to return again –
Read from the back-page of a paper, say,
Held by a neighbor in a subway train,
How at the corner of this avenue
And such a street (so are the papers filled)
A hurrying man – who happened to be you –
At noon today had happened to be killed,
I could not cry aloud – I could not cry
Aloud, or wring my hands in such a place –
I should but watch the station lights rush by
With a more careful interest on my face,
Or raise my eyes and read with greater care
Where to store furs and how to treat the hair.

Edna St Vincent Millay

Extract C

This extract is taken from the play *Romeo and Juliet* by William Shakespeare (1564–1616). Unknown to their feuding families, Juliet and Romeo have married and spent the night together, but Romeo has been banished from Verona because he killed a member of Juliet's family. So they must part.

Juliet: Wilt thou be gone? It is not yet near day:
It was the nightingale, and not the lark,
That pierced the fearful hollow of thine ear;
Nightly she sings on yon pomegranate tree:
Believe me, love, it was the nightingale.

Romeo: It was the lark, the herald of the morn,
No nightingale. Look, love, what envious streaks
Do lace the severing clouds in yonder east.
Night's candles are burnt out, and jocund day
Stands tiptoe on the misty mountain tops.
I must be gone and live, or stay and die.

Juliet: Yon light is not daylight; I know it, I.
It is some meteor that the sun exhales
To be to thee this night a torch-bearer,
And light thee on thy way to Mantua.
Therefore stay yet. Thou need'st not to be gone.

Romeo: Let me be ta'en, let me be put to death;
I am content, so thou wilt have it so.
I'll say yon grey is not the morning's eye,
'Tis but the pale reflex of Cynthia's brow;
Nor that is not the lark, whose notes do beat
The vaulty heaven so high above our heads:
I have more care to stay than will to go.
Come, death, and welcome; Juliet wills it so.
How is't, my soul? Let's talk; It is not day.

Juliet: It is, it is! Hie hence, be gone, away!
It is the lark that sings so out of tune,
Straining harsh discords and unpleasing sharps.
Some say the lark makes sweet division;
This doth not so, for she divideth us.
Some say the lark and loathed toad change eyes;
O now I would they had changed voices too,
Since arm from arm that voice doth us affray,
Hunting thee hence with hunt's-up to the day.
O, now be gone; more light and light it grows.

Romeo: More light and light; more dark and dark our woes.

Extract D

This extract is taken from *The Woodlanders* (1887) written by Thomas Hardy (1840–1928). Melbury had promised his daughter Grace to Giles Winterborne, but she rejects him and marries the new doctor. A poor villager, Marty South, had always loved Giles but he did not reciprocate her feelings, although he was kind to her. When the doctor was unfaithful, Grace turned to Giles who let her sleep in his house during stormy weather. He slept outside, fell ill and died. In this extract, which is the end of the novel, Grace's father has discovered that she has returned to her husband.

Melbury now returned to the room, and the men having declared themselves refreshed they all started on the homeward journey, which was by no means cheerless under the rays of the high moon. Having to walk the whole distance they came by a footpath rather shorter than the highway, though difficult except to those who knew the country well. This brought them by way of the church: and passing the graveyard they observed as they talked a motionless figure standing by the gate.

'I think it was Marty South,' said the hollow-tuner parenthetically.

'I think 'twas; 'a was always a lonely maid,' said Upjohn. And they passed on homeward, and thought of the matter no more.

It was Marty, as they had supposed. That evening had been the particular one of the week upon which Grace and herself had been accustomed to privately deposit flowers on Giles's grave, and this was the first occasion since his death eight months earlier on which Grace had failed to keep her appointment. Marty had waited in the road just outside Melbury's, where her fellow-pilgrim had been wont to join her, till she was weary; and at last, thinking that Grace had missed her, and gone on alone, she followed the way to the church, but saw no Grace in front of her. It got later, and Marty continued her walk till she reached the churchyard gate; but still no Grace. Yet her sense of comradeship would not allow her to go on to the grave alone, and still thinking the delay had been unavoidable she stood there with her little basket of flowers in her clasped hands, and her feet chilled by the damp ground, till more than two hours had passed. She then heard the footsteps of Melbury's men, who presently passed on their return from the search. In the silence of the night Marty could not help hearing fragments of their conversation, from which she acquired a general idea of what had occurred, and that Mrs Fitzpiers was by that time in the arms of another man than Giles.

Immediately they had dropped down the hill she entered the churchyard, going to a secluded corner behind the bushes where rose the unadorned stone that marked the last bed of Giles Winterborne. As this solitary and silent girl stood there in the moonlight, a straight slim figure, clothed in a plaitless gown, the contours of womanhood so undeveloped as to be scarcely perceptible in her, the marks of poverty and toil effaced by the misty hour, she touched sublimity at points, and looked almost like a being who had rejected with indifference the attribute of sex for the loftier quality of abstract humanism. She stooped down and cleared away the withered flowers that Grace and herself had laid there the previous week, and put her fresh ones in their place.

'Now, my own, own love,' she whispered, 'you are mine, and only mine; for she has forgot 'ee at last, although for her you died! But I – whenever I get up I'll think of 'ee, and whenever I lie down I'll think of 'ee again. Whenever I plant the young larches I'll think that none can plant as you planted; and whenever I split a gad, and whenever I turn the cider wring, I'll say none could do it like you. If ever I forget your name let me forget home and heaven! … But no, no, my love, I never can forget 'ee; for you was a good man, and did good things!'

END OF EXTRACTS

The mark scheme

Question 1

Read the two poems (Extracts A and B) carefully. They were written at different times by different writers. Basing your answer on the two poems and, where appropriate, on your wider reading in the poetry of love, compare the ways the two poets have used poetic form, structure and language to express their thoughts and ideas.

Focus

- Sonnet by Drayton
- Sonnet by Millay
- Wider reading in love poetry

Key words in the question

Two poems, wider reading, compare, ways use, form, structure, language, thoughts and ideas

Assessment grid

	Assessment Objectives			
	AO1	**AO2**	**AO3**	**AO4**
	Articulate creative, informed and relevant responses to literary texts, using appropriate terminology and concepts, and coherent, accurate written expression	Demonstrate detailed critical understanding in analysing the ways in which structure, form and language shape meanings in literary texts	Explore connections and comparisons between different literary texts, informed by interpretations of other readers	Demonstrate understanding of the significance and influence of the contexts in which literary texts are written and received
Band 1 **0–13**	Candidates characteristically: a communicate limited knowledge and understanding **of the thoughts and ideas in the two sonnets** b make few uses of appropriate terms or examples to support their **basic** interpretations **of the two sonnets** c attempt to communicate using inaccurate language d offer an unclear line of argument with poor deployment of knowledge e assert their ideas.	Candidates characteristically: a identify few aspects of structure, form and language in **the two sonnets** b may assert some aspects of vocabulary with reference to how they shape meaning c make little sense of the **ways Drayton and Millay use** form, structure and language.	Candidates characteristically: a make few links and connections between **the two sonnets**, referring to superficial features b may also make few links to **wider reading**.	Candidates characteristically: a communicate limited understanding of **17th and 20th-century** context and its influence; may address sub-genre of **sonnet** b show very little awareness of significance of relevant contextual factors on **Drayton** or **Millay** and/or responses to them.

	Candidates characteristically:	Candidates characteristically:	Candidates characteristically:	Candidates characteristically:
Band 2 **14–21**	a communicate knowledge and some understanding of **the thoughts and ideas in the two sonnets** b present responses making use of appropriate terminology and examples to support interpretations c communicate content and meaning using straightforward language accurately d adopt a generalised approach to **the two sonnets.**	a identify some aspects of structure, form or language in **the two sonnets** b describe specific aspects – **probably language and structure** – with reference to how they shape meaning c make general reference to **the ways Drayton and Millay use language, form and structure** to support their responses.	a make straightforward links and connections between the **two sonnets and note a few comparisons** b can also make a few **connections to their wider reading which may inform their interpretations.**	a comment on some of the relationships between **the two sonnets** and their **17th and 20th-century** contexts b comment on how development of the **sonnet through time** influences the reading of the **two poems.**
Band 3 **22–31**	a communicate relevant knowledge and understanding of **the thoughts and feelings expressed in the two sonnets** b present relevant responses using appropriate terminology and examples to support informed interpretations **of the poems, and successfully integrating quotation** c structure and organise their writing so that it is increasingly coherent, developing a clear line of argument d communicate content and meaning through expressive and accurate writing.	a identify relevant aspects of form, structure and language in **the two sonnets** b explore **the ways Drayton and Millay use** specific aspects to shape meaning c refer in some detail to **the two sonnets** to support their responses, showing detailed understanding of the writers' techniques.	a make systematic **comparisons between the two sonnets** b explore links and connections between the **two sonnets and some wider reading.**	a communicate understanding of relationships between **the two sonnets and their literary and historical contexts** b evaluate the influence of **17th and 20th-century context**, as well as **development of sub-genre of sonnet** on the ways in which **the two sonnets** were written and were – and are – received.
Band 4 **32–40**	a communicate detailed knowledge and understanding of **the thoughts and feelings expressed in the two sonnets** b create and sustain well organised and coherent arguments, using appropriate terminology to support informed interpretations **of the two sonnets** c structure and organise their writing using an appropriate critical register d communicate content and meaning through sophisticated, cogent, and coherent writing.	a identify significant aspects of **the ways Drayton and Millay use** structure, form and language in **the two sonnets** b explore confidently through detailed, sophisticated and mature critical analysis how **Drayton and Millay use** these aspects to create meaning c make detailed reference to texts and sources to support their responses, skilfully integrating quotation.	a analyse and evaluate connections and points of **comparison** between **the two sonnets** b explore in some detail the **connections with wider reading in love poetry.**	a explore and analyse the significance of the relationships between **the two sonnets** and their contexts, making sophisticated connections b evaluate the influence of **17th and 20th-century contexts** and **development of sub-genre of sonnet** on the ways in which literary texts were written and were – and are – received.

Question 2

Write a comparison of the ways Shakespeare and Hardy present the partings of people who love each other. You should consider:

▦ the ways the writers' choices of form, structure and language shape your responses to these extracts

▦ how your wide reading in the literature of love has contributed to your understanding and interpretation of the extracts.

Focus

▦ Extract from *Romeo and Juliet*
▦ Extract from *The Woodlanders*

Key words in the question

Comparison, ways present, partings, ways writers' choices shape responses, how wide reading contributed to understanding and interpretation

Assessment grid

	Assessment Objectives			
	AO1	**AO2**	**AO3**	**AO4**
	Articulate creative, informed and relevant responses to literary texts, using appropriate terminology and concepts, and coherent, accurate written expression	Demonstrate detailed critical understanding in analysing the ways in which structure, form and language shape meanings in literary texts	Explore connections and comparisons between different literary texts, informed by interpretations of other readers	Demonstrate understanding of the significance and influence of the contexts in which literary texts are written and received
Band 1 **0–13**	Candidates characteristically: a communicate limited knowledge and understanding of **extracts from *Romeo and Juliet* and *The Woodlanders* and focus on partings** b make few uses of appropriate terminology or examples to support their interpretations c attempt to communicate using inaccurate language d offer unclear lines of argument and unsupported assertion.	Candidates characteristically: a identify few aspects of structure, form or language in **the two extracts** b assert some aspects with reference to how they shape meaning c make limited references to **the two extracts and pay little attention to ways uses**.	Candidates characteristically: a make few **comparisons** between **the extracts from *Romeo and Juliet* and *The Woodlanders*** referring to superficial features b make few links and connections between **the two extracts and wider reading** c reflect views expressed in other interpretations or readings. d assert a narrow range of meaning.	Candidates characteristically: a communicate a limited understanding of **Shakespearean and Victorian** context and its influence on **the two extracts**.

Band 2 **14–21**	Candidates characteristically: a communicate knowledge and some understanding of **the extracts from** *Romeo and Juliet* and *The Woodlanders* and focus on partings b present responses making use of appropriate terminology and examples to support their interpretations c communicate content and meaning using straightforward language accurately d adopt a generalised approach.	Candidates characteristically: a identify some aspects of **the ways Shakespeare and Hardy use** structure, form or language in **these two extracts to present partings** b comment on specific aspects **of the two extracts** with reference to how they shape meaning c make some reference to the extracts to support their responses d show general awareness of **Shakespeare's and Hardy's** techniques.	Candidates characteristically: a note comparisons between **the two extracts in terms of presentation of partings** b make links and connections between **the two extracts and their wider reading in the literature of love** c communicate reasonable understanding of views expressed in other interpretations or readings.	Candidates characteristically: a comment on some of the relationships between **the two extracts** and their contexts b comment on how **16th and 19th-century** culture and historical period, **drama and novel genre** influence the reading of **the two extracts**, making some appropriate connection.
Band 3 **22–31**	Candidates characteristically: a communicate relevant knowledge and understanding of **the extracts from** *Romeo and Juliet* and *The Woodlanders* and the focus on partings b present relevant responses using appropriate terminology and examples to support informed responses c structure and organise increasingly coherent writing, integrating quotations from the texts d communicate content and meaning through well-controlled and accurate writing.	Candidates characteristically: a identify relevant aspects of form, structure and language in **the two extracts** b explore **the ways Shakespeare and Hardy** use specific aspects to shape meaning c refer in detail to **the two extracts and to appropriate sources from their wider reading** to support their responses.	Candidates characteristically: a explore **comparisons between the two extracts** in a systematic way b explore links and connections between the **two extracts and their wider reading in the literature of love** c show clear understanding of views expressed in other interpretations or readings.	Candidates characteristically: a communicate understanding of relationships between **the two extracts** and their contexts b evaluate the influence of **16th and 19th-century** culture and historical period, and of the **drama and novel genre** on the ways in which literary texts were written and were – and are – received.
Band 4 **32–40**	Candidates characteristically: a communicate detailed knowledge and understanding of **the two extracts from** *Romeo and Juliet* and *The Woodlanders* and the focus on partings b create and sustain well organised and coherent arguments, using appropriate terminology to support informed interpretations c structure and organise their writing using an appropriate critical register, and integrating appropriate quotations d communicate content and meaning through sophisticated, cogent and coherent writing.	Candidates characteristically: a identify significant aspects of structure, form and language in **the two extracts** b explore confidently through detailed and sophisticated critical analysis **the ways Shakespeare and Hardy** use these aspects to create meaning c make reference in detail to **the two extracts and to appropriate sources from their wider reading** to support their responses.	Candidates characteristically: a analyse and evaluate points of comparison between **the two extracts** b explore connections between **the two extracts and their wider reading in the literature of love** c engage sensitively with mature and informed understanding with different readings and interpretations.	Candidates characteristically: a explore and analyse the significance of the relationships between **the two extracts** and their contexts, making sophisticated comparisons b evaluate the influence of **16th and 19th-century** culture and historical period, and of the **drama and novel** genre on the ways in which literary texts were written and were – and are – received.

Summary

This chapter has shown you the importance of:

- linking all your resources and preparation in order to answer the paper
- making up your own questions
- looking carefully at the criteria in the marking grid in order to have maximum success.

Conclusion

If you have worked through this book and taken our advice, we are confident that you will have grown into an **informed, autonomous reader** who has every chance of success in the examination.

Glossary

A

Active creator: a maker of meaning; a reader who has individual ideas rather than re-cycling the ideas of others.

Allegory: extended metaphor that veils a moral or political underlying meaning.

Alliteration: repetition of the initial letter or sound in adjacent words to create an atmospheric or onomatopoeic effect, e.g. 'she sells sea shells'.

Allusion: passing reference to another literary work.

Ambiguity: capacity of words to have two simultaneous meanings, in the context as a device for enriching meaning.

Anachronism: chronological misplacing of person, event or object.

Analogy: perception of similarity between two things.

Antithesis: contrasting of ideas by balancing words or phrases of opposite meaning.

Assonance: repetition of a vowel sound in words in close proximity.

Autonomy: independence and confidence in making meaning from texts.

B

Ballad: narrative poem in short, rhymed verses, usually telling of love, the supernatural and travel.

Bathos: sudden change of register from the sublime to the ridiculous.

Biography: account of an individual's life written by someone else.

Blank verse: unrhymed iambic pentameter, the staple form of Shakespeare plays.

Burlesque: incongruous and ludicrous dramatic imitation for comic or satirical effect.

C

Caesura: deliberate break or pause in a line of poetry, signified by punctuation.

Canon: approved traditional literary works to be found on academic syllabuses.

Colloquial: informal language of conversational speech.

Comedy: Ancient Greek form of drama in which confusions and deceptions are unravelled, with amusement along the way, ending in resolution, restitution and reconciliation; play with happy ending.

Conceit: an extended simile.

Connotations: associations evoked by a word.

Contextuality: historical, social and cultural background of a text.

Couplet: two consecutive lines of poetry that are paired in rhyme.

Courtly love: a literary convention going back to the Middle Ages; a knight serves his lady according to a well-defined ritual and code of conduct.

D

Diction: choice of words; vocabulary from a particular semantic field.

Dramatic irony: when the audience knows something the character speaking does not, which creates humour or tension.

E

Elegy: lament for the death or permanent loss of someone or something.

Epic: long narrative poem telling a tale of heroic achievements over a period of time, often related to national identity and with supernatural elements.

Epistolary: taking the form of letters or exchange of letters.

Euphemism: tactful word or phrase to refer to something unpleasant or offensive.

F

Free verse: poetry without a regular metrical pattern or rhyme.

G

Genre: type or form of writing with identifiable characteristics; the three main literary genres are prose, poetry and drama; there are also sub-genres.

H

Heroic couplets: iambic pentameter rhymed in pairs; used in epic and mock heroic poetry.

Hyperbole: deliberate exaggeration for effect.

I

Imagery: descriptive language appealing to the senses; may be sustained or recurring throughout texts, usually in the form of simile or metaphor.

Informed response: a reading of a text based on knowledge and understanding.

Intertextuality: relationship between one text and another.

Irony: language intended to mean the opposite of the words expressed; or amusing or cruel reversal of an outcome expected, intended or deserved.

Lyric: expression of strong feelings, usually love; suggestive of music.

Magic realism: 20th-century description of a work that interweaves realistic details with supernatural and dream-like mythical elements in an everyday setting.

Melodrama: sensational play with stereotyped characters, popular in the 19th century.

Metaphor: suppressed comparison implied not stated, e.g. 'the bishop was a pillar of the church'.

Metaphysical: a school of 17th-century poets known for their far-fetched imagery and witty, imaginative and intellectual comparisons.

Mock heroic: using epic/heroic style for trivial events in order to ridicule both.

Mystery plays: religious plays acted out of doors, telling the history of the world from the Creation to the Last Judgement.

Ode: lengthy lyrical and reflective poem addressed to the subject.

Onomatopoeia: words that imitate the sound being described, e.g. bang, smash.

Ottava rima: a stanza of eight lines.

Oxymoron: two contradictory terms united in a single phrase, e.g. 'bitter sweet'.

Pageant: spectacle or play about the history of a place, performed in the open, sometimes in procession.

Parody: imitation and exaggeration of style for the purpose of humour and ridicule.

Pastoral: simple, innocent and idyllic rural existence among shepherds, deriving from the golden age of Arcadia in Ancient Greece.

Pathetic fallacy: attributing emotions to inanimate objects, usually elements of nature, to represent the persona's feelings, e.g. describing the weather as stormy when a character is distressed.

Personification: human embodiment of an abstraction or object, using a capital letter or he or she.

Picaresque: narrative dealing with criminal and/or low-life characters on a journey of some kind.

Polemic: a controversial discussion.

Protagonist: principal characters in a drama or literary work.

Quatrain: four-lined stanza or group of four lines distinguished by a rhyme scheme.

Realism: the presentation of life as it is, rather than in a glamorous or romantic way.

Rhetoric: art of persuasion using emotive language and stylistic devices.

Rhyme: repetition of a vowel sound in words at the end of lines.

Rhythm: pace and sound pattern of writing, created by metre, vowel length, syntax and punctuation.

Satire: exposing of vice or foolishness of a person or institution to ridicule.

Simile: comparison introduced by 'as' or 'like'; epic simile is a lengthy and detailed analogy.

Sonnet: lyrical poem of 14 lines of rhymed iambic pentameter, either an octet and sestet (Petrarchan) or three quatrains and a couplet (Shakespearean) or 14 lines ending with a couplet (Miltonic).

Stanza: another term for a verse; there are various forms depending on the number of lines and type of rhyme scheme.

Stream of consciousness: a method used by some modern novelists (e.g. Joyce) to relate the innermost thoughts and feelings of characters without logical sequence, syntax or, sometimes, punctuation.

Symbol: an object, person or event that represents something more than itself.

Tragedy: play or literary work of a predominantly sorrowful nature, traditionally concerning kings or rulers, having a disastrous and fatal conclusion; characterised by waste, loss and a fall from power.

English Literature through time grid

Century	Period/monarch	Genres/writers	Commentary	Critical theory
14th and 15th	Richard II 1377–99 Medieval Gothic	Mystery/morality plays Tales Epic prose Chaucer 1343–1400 Malory 1400–71	Key features – chivalric romances (King Arthur) and mystery/morality plays Key texts – *Canterbury Tales* (Chaucer) and *Le Morte d'Arthur* (Malory) Influence of printing press 1474	
16th and 17th	Renaissance Henry VIII 1509–47 Elizabethan Elizabeth I 1558–1603	Tragedies, comedies, sonnets, classical verse, allegorical poetry Spenser 1552–99 Sidney 1554–86 Shakespeare 1564–1616 Marlowe 1564–93 Jonson 1572–1637	Drama becomes important; London playhouses Masque and spectacle popular Also courtly love poetry Monarchs themselves were writers	Sidney *Apology for Poetry* 1595
	Jacobean James I 1603–25	Metaphysical poetry, revenge tragedy Donne 1572–1631 Webster 1580–1625	Middle of 17th century metaphysical poetry	
	Caroline Charles I 1625–49	Restoration drama, social comedy	Charles 1 executed 1649	Dryden *Essay on Dramatic Poesy* 1668
	Commonwealth 1649–60 Civil War	Milton 1608–74 Marvell 1621–78	Puritans closed theatres	
	Restoration Charles II 1660–85	Restoration drama, social comedy Wycherley 1640–1716 Congreve 1670–1729	Theatres reopened 1660 – comedy of manners. Influence of court on drama and poetry – bawdy, cynical, amoral	
18th	Regency Anne, George I and II 1700–60	Satire, epic, political essays, epistolary and picaresque novels, bawdy verse Defoe 1660–1731 Swift 1667–1745 Pope 1688–1744 Fielding 1707–54 Johnson 1709–84	New genre of novel in early 1700s with Defoe Popularity of biting satire, attacking those in power By end of period 3-volume confessional, satirical or picaresque novels well established – as well as the romantic novels to cater for female readership; importance of lending libraries Blake precursor of Romantic movement with interest in childhood and individual	Johnson *Lives of the Poets* 1779
	Augustan (Enlightenment) George III 1760–1820	Blake 1757–1827		
	Romantic I	Lyric poetry, gothic poetry and prose, narrative poetry, Romantic novels Wordsworth 1770–1850 Scott 1771–1832 Coleridge 1776 –1849 Austen 1775 –1817	First generation of Romantic writers Passion and imagination in literature, especially poetry Influence of Middle Ages and Gothic era in settings, plots and characters Reaction against previous period – importance of rebellion and independence Worship of Nature in all aspects	Wordsworth *Preface to Lyrical Ballads* 1800 Coleridge *Biographia Literaria* 1817

19th	Romantic II George IV 1820–37	Byron 1788–1824 P. Shelley 1792–1822 Keats 1795–1821 M. Shelley 1791–1851	Second generation of Romantics	Shelley *Defence of Poetry* 1821
	Victorian Industrial Revolution Victoria 1837–1901 Pre–Raphaelite	Serial novels, political, patriotic, religious verse, social and industrial novels Gaskell 1810–65 C. Brontë 1816–55 E. Brontë 1818–48 George Eliot 1819–55 Barrett Browning 1806–61 Tennyson 1809–92 Dickens 1812–70 Robert Browning 1812–89 Hardy 1840–1928 Wilde 1856–1900 Yeats 1865–1939	Themes of duty, nationalism and trade, education and morality until World War One Class and gender divide Family values – happy domesticity – woman as angel of the house Effect of Darwin on ideas Wide reading public – serialisation, e.g. Dickens More restrained than Romantics but still preoccupied with countryside, children and feelings	Hazlitt *Lectures on the English Poets* 1818 **Liberal Humanism** Matthew Arnold *Culture and Anarchy* 1869
20th	Edwardian Edward VII 1901–10	War poetry, psychological novels, symbolist novels, short stories Wells 1866–1946 E. Thomas 1878–1917 Sassoon 1886–1967 Owen 1893–1918 E.M. Forster 1879–1970	First half of 20th century, World War One brought upheaval and questioning of all aspects of life – rupture with past and its beliefs, e.g. heroes Writers turned to art – art for art's sake Interest in theory, experimentalism and breaking rules	
	Modernism George V 1910–36 George VI 1936–52	Science fiction Stream of consciousness novel Woolf 1882–1941 Joyce 1882–1941 Lawrence 1885–1930 Socialist poetry and fiction T.S. Eliot 1888–1965 Beckett 1906–89 Auden 1907–73	New genres of science fiction and psychological novel sprang from preoccupation with social and personal identity Writer alienated from society Influence of Freudian psychology – exploring the workings of the unconscious; fascination for sexual fantasy, mysticism and use of symbols Traditional chronological narrative replaced by connotation, association and use of symbols Recognition of instability and complexity of personality Concept of epiphany Growth of feminist writing	**The New Practical Criticism** T.S. Eliot 1920s I.A. Richards *Practical Criticism* 1924 W. Empson *Seven Types of Ambiguity* 1930 F.R. Leavis *The Common Pursuit* 1952 **Formalism**
	Post-modernism Elizabeth II 1952–	Post-modern novel Political and social poetry and drama Kitchen sink drama Drama of the absurd Post-colonial and feminist poetry, prose and drama Tennessee Williams 1911–83 Larkin 1922–85 Friel 1929– Hughes 1930–98 Plath 1932–63 Stoppard 1937– Atwood 1939– Heaney 1939– Walker 1944– McEwan 1948– Duffy 1955–	From 1960s to present, preoccupations of modernism shared but taken further Traditional linear narrative mocked and rejected and comfort of closure rejected Randomness, discontinuity and contradiction, pastiche and deliberate irony Makes us reflect on act of writing and relationship between writer, character, and reader Parallelism, binary opposition, doublings, mixing fictional and historical characters, twisting well-known myths	**Structuralism** **Post-structuralism** **New Historicism** **Cultural Materialism** **Marxist** **Psychoanalytical** **Feminist** **Post-colonial**

Index

Entries in **bold** are key terms and are also in the glossary on pages 122–3

Acknowledgements

The authors and publishers wish to thank the following for permission to use copyright material:

A&C Black Publishers for extracts from Bertolt Brecht, *The Caucasian Chalk Circle*, Methuen Drama (1988) pp25, 93–95; Faber and Faber Ltd for extracts from Sylvia Plath, 'Morning Song' in *Collected Poems* by Sylvia Plath (2002); Thom Gunn, 'Terminal' in *The Man with Night Sweats* by Thom Gunn (1992); Brian Friel, from *Translations* (1981) Act 3, Scene 2; Harold Pinter, *Betrayal* (1991); and Wendy Cope 'Spared' in *Two Cures for Love: Selected Poems 1979–2006* by Wendy Cope (2008); W.H. Auden, 'Stop all the clocks, cut off the telephone'; David Higham Associates on behalf of the author for an extract from Elizabeth Jennings, 'Friends' in *The Secret Brother* by Elizabeth Jennings, Macmillan (1966); W.W. Norton & Company Ltd for e e cummings, 'my sweet old etcetera' in *Complete Poems 1904–1962* by e e cummings, edited by George J. Firmage. Copyright © 1991 the Trustees for the e e cummings Trust and George James Firmage; The Society of Authors as the Literary Representative of the Estate of the author for an extract from Virginia Woolf, *To The Lighthouse*, Wordsworth Classics (1994), pp28–9; The Arthur Waley Estate for 'Plucking the Rushes', translated by Arthur Waley in *170 Chinese Poems*, Constable & Co Ltd (1919). Copyright © The Arthur Waley Estate; A.P. Watt Ltd on behalf of Gráinne Yeats for W.B. Yeats, 'When you are old'; Amber Lane Press for an extract from Martin Sherman, *Bent* (1979) pp77–80. Copyright © Martin Sherman 1979; Elizabeth Barnett, Literary Executor of the Edna St Vincent Millay Society for an extract from Edna St Vincent Millay, 'If I should learn, in some quite casual way!' Copyright © 1917, 1945 Edna St Vincent Millay.

p20 © Portrait of Lord Byron (1788–1824) (oil on canvas) by Philips, Thomas (1770–1845), Private Collection/The Bridgeman Art Library; p21 © Burstein Collection/Corbis; p23 © Donald Cooper/Photostage; p28 Copyright © Christie's Images Ltd; p30 Copyright © Christie's Images Ltd; p33 © Stapleton Collection/Corbis; p35 Credit: The Hireling Shepherd, 1951 (oil on canvas) by Hunt, William Holman (1827–1910) © Manchester Art Gallery, UK/The Bridgeman Art Library; p37 © The Gallery Collection/Corbis; p40 Credit: Planetary orbits, plate 18 from 'The Celestial Atlas, or the Harmony of the Universe' (Atlas coelestis seu harmonia macrocosmica) depicting the Ptolemaic and Tycho Brahe systems, pub. by Joannes Janssonius, Amsterdam, 1660–1 (engraving) by Cellarius, Andreas (17th century) (after), Private Collection/The Bridgeman Art Library; p47 Copyright © Christie's Images Ltd; p56 © Woodfall/The Kobal Collection; p60 Credit: Portrait of Mary Wollstonecraft (1759–97) c.1793 (oil on canvas) by Keenan, John (fl.1791–1815), Private Collection/The Bridgeman Art Library; p65 Credit: The Kiss, 1907–08 (oil on canvas) by Klimt, Gustav (1862–1918) Osterreichische Galerie Belvedere, Vienna, Austria/The Bridgeman Art Library; p66 © Bettmann/Corbis; p71 © VIC/APPIA/The Kobal Collection; p79 © Focus Features/The Kobal Collection/Bailey, Alex; p83 © V&A Images; p84 © Sandro Vannini/Corbis; p86 © Donald Cooper/Photostage; p88 © Lebrecht Music & Arts 2002–2007; p93 © Jeremy Hoare/Alamy; p94 © Donald Cooper/Photostage; p99 © Donald Cooper/Photostage.